NEW FOR THE '80s—
TOGETHERNESS IS BACK
AND BETTER THAN EVER!

This is not a book about "open marriage" or "creative divorce." It is a book about YOU—the individual—but not some YOU out in space with no earthly ties.

After all, if you are "your own best friend," who is this person you find sharing your home, your bed, and your future?

During her 25 years of marriage counseling, Marlene LaRoe has heard from husbands and wives in every stage of marriage. She has learned what works and what doesn't. She had discovered the ways that YOU can preserve a loving, mutually satisfying marriage.

She shows exactly what can ruin a marriage when you least expect it—how to deal with it, and how to make your love grow through the predictable crises of married life.

HOW NOT TO RUIN A PERFECTLY GOOD MARRIAGE!

Marlene Shelton LaRoe
with Lee Herrick

BANTAM BOOKS

TORONTO · NEW YORK · LONDON

HOW NOT TO RUIN A PERFECTLY GOOD MARRIAGE

*A Bantam Book / published by arrangement with
Follett Publishing Company*

PRINTING HISTORY

Follett edition published August 1979

Serialized in Cosmopolitan, *April 1980 issue;
and in* New Woman, *May, 1980 issue*

Bantam edition / August 1980

Contents

Acknowledgments

This book would not have been possible without the courageous thinking of those who have influenced both my counseling and my living. To these individuals, I wish to acknowledge my sincere gratitude.

To Dr. Harry Stack Sullivan, who was a true pioneer in understanding the developmental phases of intimacy that I discuss in chapter 1; and the delicate balance among sex, intimacy, and security, which is the focus of chapter 3.

To Erik Erikson, whose theories concerning the crises, or turning points, in adulthood stimulated my thinking on the development of the marriage relationship.

To Anne Morrow Lindbergh, whose *Gift from the Sea* has been my constant companion throughout my adult life.

To Dr. Paul Tillich, whose *Courage to Be* has provided continual professional insight and personal inspiration.

To Dr. Rupert Koeninger, my lifelong mentor, who taught me to walk in the other man's moccasins.

To Annette Garrett, my professor at Smith College of Social Work, whose belief in me and my abilities as a therapist inspires me to continued growth and knowledge to this day.

And finally, to my friend, teacher, and lover: my husband, Dr. DeWitt Shelton, who has encouraged me always to reach and stretch; and to, above all else, be honest with myself and others.

HOW NOT TO RUIN
A
PERFECTLY
GOOD
MARRIAGE!

Introduction

I've read all the books. I know all about "open marriage" and "creative divorce." I've learned about "pairing" and the "joy of sex." I can "say no" without flinching. And I can locate my "erroneous zones" blindfolded.

But a few puzzling questions still remain. If I am now my "own best friend," then who is this man I find sharing my home, my bed, and my future? Where does he fit in? While I'm doing all this "passaging" and "shifting gears," what's he up to? What are *we* up to as a couple? How are we changing—for better or worse? How are we growing—together or apart? What are we doing right? But more importantly, where are we going wrong?

How *do* we (meaning now close to half of us who step up to the altar these days) go about ruining a perfectly good marriage anyway?

In my twenty-five years as a marriage counselor, I've discovered some ingenious answers! But for the most part, I have found that we all have a few standard ploys—from protecting to pretending to just plain loafing—that can cut us off from the friendship, the intimacy, the security we seek and need in this most important of all human relationships.

Certainly, books have been written all around marriage, how to do it and how to undo it. But little has been written about how to keep it, care for it, nurture it. As with virtually any growth process, there are common patterns and problems. And there are both creative and destructive ways to resolve and learn from these problems.

In this book, I would like to share some of these ways with you. You might think of it as a type of reference book for the married—a book to help couples understand what is normal development, what problems to expect, how to deal with these problems, and when to call for help.

It is not an easy task, this care and feeding of the couple, for it involves not just the growth—painful, rewarding, and necessary—of one human being but of two. But it is an essential one, for it is this primal connection, the couple, that satisfies our most basic needs for closeness, for belonging.

Feelings of isolation and compartmentalization spawned by the urban, mobile society in which we live increase our need for a relationship that gives us this sense of belonging. Two by two we go today, just the two of us and our children (and fewer and fewer of these!). So the marriage relationship becomes increasingly valuable as we seek to share in a thing of meaning, to experience a sense of real closeness to another person.

I do not think that this need for closeness is cultural. I think it is a basic animal need. In the absence of this closeness, we feel loneliness and desolation. We may fill our lives with work, religion, sex, children. But without this intimate relationship, the emptiness remains.

What does it take to develop this intimate relationship in marriage? How do we get it? How do we keep it? In a word: work.

Work is nothing new to us. We *believe* in it. It is

part of our heritage and our hope. We believe in learning and practice and effort—and reward. And that belief puts something more, something better, within the reach of almost everyone. So we gladly accept that it takes work to become a good baseball player or teacher or mechanic or artist.

Yet who would think of adding husband or wife to that list? Rare indeed is the person who accepts—or even wants to consider the possibility!—that marriage takes work too, that it requires learning and practicing certain skills to make it valuable and pleasurable and good.

Why? Because we believe in something else just as strongly as we believe in work. We believe in Love—the Love that knows no bounds; that conquers all; that makes everything else easy, natural, instinctive. We believe—quite innocently, hopefully, and blindly—that Love is enough.

It isn't.

To anyone who is, or ever has been, married, that bit of truth probably doesn't come as news. It's usually one of the first things we find out in fact. What we *don't* find out is what to *do* about it and how.

And that is what this book is about. We must begin by accepting that we have to learn how to be married, just as we have to learn how to practice law or teach school or tune an engine. We must learn how to be loving toward those we love. We must learn how to share, how to care, how to have good sex. None of these things are nearly as natural or instinctive as we would like to believe—fortunately.

If work gives all of us a shot at success in baseball or business or whatever we may want and choose, it also gives us an opportunity for success in marriage that love alone never could. It doesn't leave this most primal relationship to chance or to fate or even to Love. It leaves it to us.

1

No Coaching from the Past, Please

Let's start with the ground rules—all those unwritten but inviolate rules for men and women, wives and husbands, that have been passed down like family heirlooms from generation to generation.

From mother to daughter:

1. *Get a man.* No self-respecting woman would be caught dead without one. HE is your ultimate goal, the only thing that stands between you and loneliness, responsibility, and, worst of all, social failure.

2. *Relinquish the reins.* HE is in charge now. Defer to his judgment. Tiptoe around his ego. And keep a sharp crease in those pants he's wearing.

3. *Make him happy.* Be whatever HE wants and needs you to be!

   Be charming. Remember, you reflect on HIM!

   Be feminine. That includes sexy. (And keep your eye on the competition!)

   Be adaptable. (Infinitely adaptable!) Leave no expectation unmet.

Be understanding. HE's had a hard day.

Be intelligent. But not too intelligent.

Be faithful. No exceptions!

4. *Be a good wife.* Just like your mother.

   Keep the house spotless. HE's got more important things to do.

   Raise perfect children. Motherhood is your noblest calling.

   Take a job if you must. But remember your priorities.

   Try to enjoy sex. If all else fails, fake it. (His ego is at stake!)

5. *Feel really guilty.* If you fall short, something must be terribly wrong with *you.*

From father to son:

1. *Make your mark.* First things first, and that means your career. Climb that ladder. Shoulder that responsibility. Tackle those long hours. Success at all costs.

2. *Get a woman.* You're going to need *help,* and she can give it. But take your time. Play the field. And choose wisely.

3. *Take the reins.* You've got two lives in your hands now, and probably more on the way. So take a firm grip. Make all important decisions. And don't get bogged down in the details of family life. You've got more important things to do.

4. *Take good care of her.* Try to give her what you know a woman needs.

   Be strong. Conceal weakness at all costs.

   Be masculine. If you must have feelings, keep them hidden.

   Be protective. Shield her from the world.

   Be intelligent. Remember, you're thinking for two.

   Be faithful. At least here in town.

5. *Be a good husband.* Just like your father.
   Keep up with the Joneses. Remember, you reflect on her!
   Empty the trash twice a week. That comes with the territory.
   Present a strong father figure. Don't get too close to the children.
   Demonstrate sexual prowess. After all, it's performance that counts!
6. *Feel slightly cheated.* If the marriage falls short, remember that wasn't your department!

These are exaggerated to be sure. But they represent the absurd extensions of the basic ground rules couples have been trying to live by for generations— rules that preserve the far more basic philosophy that underpins, and often undermines, the relationship between two people.

1. *Play it safe.* The stakes are high in this game, so don't take any chances. Keep your feelings close to your chest. And never, *never* go for broke. You might lose everything.
2. *Keep a trick or two up your sleeve.* If winning isn't everything, losing is nothing. So keep unpleasant truths to yourself. Pretend that you've got something you don't. And if all else fails, fake it.
3. *Stick to the rule book.* No additions or deletions, please. If it was good enough for Mom and Dad, it's good enough for you.
4. *Put your feet up.* You're in this game till death do you part. So go ahead and take it easy. Relax. Nobody is going anywhere.

These are just for starters. The intricate details, the nuances, the protocols, the rules that have governed couples' lives together are endless.

Needless to say, the old rules aren't faring too well. Current odds still favor marriage over divorce by a slight margin, but the odds are narrowing steadily. Too much has happened to the world, to people—the Pill, mobility, women's rights, men's rights, the sixties, the economy—to keep relationships confined to the old gameboard.

REWRITING THE RULE BOOK

So people are writing their own rules, experimenting with alternatives to the old game plan. They're living together, signing contracts, and "opening" marriages. They're trying to find a workable, livable, meaningful way to establish and nurture the relationship between two people that we think of as marriage, official or unofficial. They're searching for the flexibility, the room, two people need to grow and express themselves as individuals. After all, it takes two individuals to "relate" in the first place, to have a relationship. The old rules stifle, even thwart, this relating process, reducing it to roles, scripts. The relationship becomes static, dying, lonely.

The new rules are simple, fostering dynamic processes: relating, growing, loving. There are no elaborate sets of dos and don'ts. There are no rules for women, no rules for men. There are simply a few basic guidelines for people, for individuals, for you. They are deceptively simple. But they are not easy to come by and even harder to stick to.

1. *Go for broke.* Refuse to settle for second best or third or fourth where your relationship is concerned. This takes a great deal of courage—courage to risk everything for the big stakes; courage to face change, growth; courage to accept loss

and defeat if necessary; courage to embrace victory.

2. *Play it straight.* Be honest. Throw away the roles, the scripts. This takes courage too. Quit pretending. Know yourself and reveal that self honestly to your partner. Banish wishful thinking. Acknowledge what *is* and work to improve it.

3. *Make your own rules.* And change them whenever they become confining. Don't be afraid to explore, to expand, to grow. Try new things, both individually and as a couple. Welcome change. It adds vitality to a relationship.

4. *Roll up your shirt sleeves.* You've got work to do. Relating is work. Growing is work. Loving is work. All of these processes involve learning and practicing certain skills day in and day out.

5. *Love each other.* Love gives us courage to live openly and honestly. It makes the work meaningful, the change purposeful. It is the process, the connection, between two people that provides the continuity for the development and expression of their relationship.

STARTING WITH YOU

As with any process, there must be a beginning. Where does love begin exactly? It begins with each of us as individuals. It begins in our capacity and, yes, our hunger for intimacy and involvement with other human beings. Just as each of us is unique, so love and its expression are unique for each couple. Comparisons are difficult, for love changes and is defined and redefined by the two individuals who make up every couple.

So let's begin with you—you who are separate, you who are different. For you are. We work hard at proving we are not different, which too often translates as "weird," "peculiar," "just a little odd." And that—heaven forbid!—means conspicuous. So we mask our differences, our uniqueness. We sport the latest styles, punctuate our conversation with the newest adjectives, and borrow approved opinions on world affairs or religion or UFOs. In short, we camouflage all those rough edges of ourselves that we don't quite know what else to do with!

Now this idea of wearing masks conjures up all sorts of images about deception, insecurity, and a host of other negative attributes that few of us would care to claim. But we've all worn them, so we're in good company. And actually they're not all bad! In a way they help us learn about ourselves. We may "try on" a variety of mannerisms, interests, jobs, friends, and even life-styles—sometimes just as readily as we might change clothes—to find the proper fit, the ones that feel right for us. It's a way of exploring ourselves.

But on the other hand, these masks stand between us and others. They make living easier, to say the least, for they help us cast people in certain molds and poke them into cubbyholes. We can't see them as they really are. But, better yet, they can't see us. To accomplish this, we mask our strengths as well as our weaknesses. And these masks distort us and our perceptions of the world. But perhaps it is only by wearing them, by living within their cramped confines, that we are ever able to tear them off and stand as we are —naked as jaybirds. It takes courage to see ourselves in this way—unadorned, vulnerable. But there's no getting around it. We are what we are. And we've got what we've got—no more, no less. But often that's more and better than we think.

Sandra is one of the most beautiful women I have ever known. She does not see herself as beautiful, however, but as rather plump, a bit on the short side, and altogether much too matronly. I have heard her complimented often, told in many ways that she was beautiful. Each compliment she rebuffs, dismissing the admirer as merely tactful or, worse yet, a liar. No amount of affirmation from others can change her image of herself.

Equally striking, Joyce basks in the many compliments she receives. Yet, in confidence, she points out that her teeth are a bit askew, her feet too large. And, isolating these features, they are. The overall effect, however, is stunning. And she knows it. She also knows that there is no point in pretending that her teeth are straight or her feet two sizes smaller. You can't fool an old fooler, so there's little point in trying. We all have our unique assets and liabilities, and both we must embrace—the former with gusto and the latter with a touch of humility, and humanity as well —for they form the inner core from which we come out to relationships with others.

LEARNING THE BASICS

This coming out is a long, slow learning process. But don't worry, you've been working on it a long time. It hinges on the development of that capacity for intimacy I mentioned earlier, and it began further back than you can remember.

It began at birth, when you needed your first sense of physical closeness, the touching and the holding. You needed the intimate cuddling, comforting, and cooing. You needed the animal warmth. If you got it, you passed the first hurdle, with little required on your part but being adorable. If you didn't, you may have difficulty enjoying physical contact in intimate relationships. This physical closeness, both then and now, gives us a source of closeness—not sexual closeness but a sense of warmth. This is what women (and more and more men!) are asking for when they say, "He [she] never touches me, kisses me, unless he [she] wants sex." That warmth, that ability to express and receive tenderness with a physical touch, is missing.

But somewhere between the ages of one and a half and three, you needed more. You needed to be seen and recognized as an individual. This "see me" stage has two major components. The first and simplest is relating to others through eye-to-eye contact. If we bypass this step, we may be in for problems like David's. David never looks at his wife, Susan, when they are talking, apparently more enamored with the water spots on the ceiling, the plant in the corner, or even the scuff marks on his shoes than with her—her face, her eyes. This makes Susan feel that she is not seen and therefore not heard, and least of all loved.

The second, and more complicated, step in this "see me" stage involves drawing the line between "me" and "them." It is during this phase that we learn to move back and forth between a totally dependent life and an independent life. At this age we are not convinced that we can move away from our parents and still find them there when we get back. Even a journey of a few feet is a very long one to such a small child. So we take a few independent steps away from Mother and turn to say, "See me! Do you see me?" Then we can continue to play on our own with the reassurance that Mother's warm lap is still in sight.

People who do not make this particular developmental hurdle often have real difficulty in not "fusing in" with their spouse in later life. Cindy is such a person. No matter what the question was—from "What movie would you like to see?" to "Do you want to make love?"—her answer was always the same: "Whatever you want to do, George, is fine with me." With no sense of being a person in her own right,

Cindy became her husband's shadow, clinging to him, smothering him. George felt burdened and did not know why. Cindy felt resentful and did not know why. As she began to understand herself, Cindy began the slow process of differentiating her needs and desires from George's. In saying, "I don't want to go to the movies. I'd rather go to the ballet," Cindy was declaring, "I am a person. See me." Relieved, George affirmed her, his words and actions saying, "Yes, I see you, Cindy, as a person separate from me with whom I can share my life."

Between ages three and five, Mom and Dad were becoming old hat, and you needed a playmate—literally, someone to play with. Some people never learn to play, have no concept of being playful. Too often they grow into the dull Jacks of the all-work-and-no-play cliché who wind up with, at best, planned spontaneity. Barry is just such a man. Sincere and caring, Barry works very hard and is always there when his wife and family need him. But he does not know how to play. Even on vacations, he is so busy making lists and itineraries and schedules for everyone else's play-time that he cannot relax. So when his wife wants to "play," she is forced to enlist the company of other couples, just so she can have someone to share the fun. A very important part of her, and of Barry, is not being shared in the relationship.

Now the next stage of development got a little trickier. You began to realize, at about age six or seven, that others had some things you wanted, and some you needed, and that it was going to take something called cooperation to get them. You may not have known what that word meant, but you knew it was important. The mother of twins told me once (when the story was old enough to be funny) of a particularly frantic day when these two preschool monsters, under coaching from their father, marched round and round her wet kitchen floor chanting, "We wanna cooperate, we wanna cooperate," convinced that it must be the greatest thing since peanut butter.

And, in a way, it is. Cooperation is the essential ingredient that gets, and keeps, two people together to solve problems in later relationships. Very simply, cooperation may be thought of as mutual back-scratching: "I'll do *this* for you [or with you] so I can get *that* for me." We cooperate with another person, do something for that person, to get something we want in return.

Every Sunday was a day of turmoil in the Miller household. Karen rose at the crack of dawn to start a big dinner so that after church the whole family could sit down to the traditional roast, potatoes, and fresh peas. She had every minute planned, from the time the alarm clock went off until the church bell rang. The only problem was that her husband, Jack, and the two children weren't cooperating. They took their time, dawdling in the bathroom and reading the Sunday comics. But they finally made it to church, with everyone upset over being rushed and Karen feeling very put upon. After the service it was rush home, change clothes, and all sit down to a beautiful meal. More problems. Jack wanted to play golf. The children wanted to go to the park and play with their friends. So self-sacrificing Karen was forced to shout that not only were they going to eat together first but do the dishes as well.

One day Jack sat down with Karen and asked, "Is Sunday dinner really so important to you?" Karen said, "Of course. We always had a big Sunday dinner when I was growing up. It was a time to be together as a family." Then Jack inquired, "Is our Sunday dinner like your dream of what it should be?" Karen had to answer, "No." As they discussed the matter, they discovered that no one, not even Karen, wanted the big Sunday meal. Instead they wanted to be freer on that day. So they decided that everyone would do his or her part—would cooperate—to make Sunday a free day. They gave up the big meal. After church everyone did as he or she pleased the rest of the day, snacking here and there whenever hungry. Karen no longer felt like a martyr. Jack and the children no longer resented her demands. Everybody got something that he or she wanted. And nobody starved.

It was through such back and forth give-and-take that you first discovered, about age eight or ten, someone who gave and took just the things you needed. And you found your first real friend—someone you shared your secrets with, your new bike, your bubble gum cards; someone you actually wrote letters to when you were on vacation; someone you could go to when you ran away from home. This is when we first learn to share our thoughts and feelings, to care what really happens to another person, and to be loyal. This is the first feeling of love, as I define it, that a child experiences. We feel genuinely close to our friend and care about his or her welfare almost as much as our own. Loyalty begins to develop in the real sense of the word. We learn that love is more valuable to us than to be loved. And the good feeling that loving our friend gives us makes us continue to love.

It is this friendship, this sharing, that is so important in a later relationship. Sharing and taking an interest in another person is what gives vitality to a relationship. How many times have I sat on each side of an imaginary fence with a couple. From strong and silent Gary I heard, "She isn't interested in what I have to say or in what I'm doing. And I don't want to burden her." While the subject of that declaration, Jean, his wife of ten years, moaned, "I never know what he's thinking, why he's upset, how he feels about his job. He doesn't trust me." Both wanted the same thing, but neither knew how to go about getting it. But the wanting was the first step. Learning was the second. It took some time, but Gary did learn to share his world with Jean—to quit cheating himself, and her, of that special closeness we know as friendship.

Now there's one more important ingredient in intimacy, the one you stirred in somewhere in your teens. And it was mighty potent. This last ingredient you added was lust. My, how we want to call it everything *but* lust. Yet it is lust, pure and simple, that opens our eyes to that wonderful half of humanity we scarcely noticed before. We develop crushes and the capacity for falling in love, which is the prelude to loving someone of the opposite sex.

At this point, I'd like to clear up one of those favorite old wives' tales that has been with us since the dawn of puppy love, one that's just about as true as all those you ever heard about warts—the one that warns us that love is blind. Now, in truth, love has 20/20 vision. If love were our guide through this phase of our development, we'd all make a lot fewer detours. Instead we usually find ourselves "falling in love," which is the next best thing to being legally blind. But it works magic!

A woman I know, who is in fact legally blind without two little spheres of brown plastic nestled in her eyes, clearly describes this type of magic. Behind those lenses the world materializes in clear focus. Suits have wrinkles, and so do faces. Ah, but *remove* them, and the lines vanish. The lights make halos. The world looks soft and faintly radiant.

It's like falling in love. Life fairly glows when we're with our beloved. He or she dominates our thoughts, our conversation, our daydreams. To be in love is to be "center stage"—to revel in our feelings, our perceptions, our vitality, our aliveness. It is a purely sexual, selfish act, for the leading role is ours. We cannot truly love the other person, for we cannot perceive him or her clearly. We see only our dream of our leading man or lady.

This blissful state may last awhile—sometimes a year, sometimes longer. But inevitably the curtain rings up on act 2. What a rude awakening when the dreams vanish, leaving only two very real people behind. It is here, if we're lucky, that love enters stage left to help us size up the situation. Hopefully, we discover beside us a best friend as well as lover—someone we care about and want to be near.

I am in no way saying, "Don't fall in love." In fact, I heartily recommend that people do it at least a dozen times as teenagers so that by the time they hit their twenties, they know the difference between lust and love. Lust is the force that catapults us into the world of male and female. But it is love that gives that world meaning. If we think that lust, with all its heart-pounding sexual fervor, is love, we are going to be badly mistaken—and sorely disappointed. Many people go through life seeking someone who gives them this "magical" feeling, divorcing many and loving none.

If we fall in and out of love many times, we learn that lust is not all that love is about. We learn that love is about friendship, as well as sex. And we begin looking for a best friend as well as bed partner. Our society makes this difficult, this being best friends with someone of the opposite sex. We are often taught to regard our spouse as an intimate enemy, not as a loved and treasured friend. But this is changing, as people like Mark and Barbara are changing.

Mark had his life neatly arranged. He had men as friends and a woman as a wife (for sex) and mother (for his children). But after fifteen years of marriage, this woman-wife-mother named Barbara turned his world upside down. She felt lonely. She felt like a sexual object. She felt that Mark did not see her as a person and friend. Desperate, she asked for a separation. For Mark, this crisis was a truly awakening experience because he had no concept of marriage outside of the traditional roles. When he had to change or lose Barbara, he began an adventure in learning about friendship, and about love.

"I never knew that this world was out here," he said, meaning, "I never knew that a man and woman could be friends." Mark is excited about getting to know Barbara as a person and learning how to share life with her. After fifteen years Mark and Barbara are at last putting together all the ingredients of intimacy and learning to truly love.

When we, as young adults, enter a truly intimate relationship, we need to have gone through all of these developmental phases. If we skipped any, we're destined to spend a lot of time and energy running back to them. If we have not had these learning experiences, like Mark and Barbara, we must learn them later. It makes the learning more difficult but certainly not impossible. This is why we need to understand what intimacy and loving are all about so that we can learn what we have missed in development.

MAKING THE BREAK

Eighteen seems to be the magic number in our society. By that time most of us have at least a rudimentary knowledge of these basics. We are by then, hopefully, well equipped for our flight from the nest—to break from our parents, to join a covey of friends for support or fly off alone to explore the outside world. Usually at this point few of us need any encouragement. In fact, we've probably been flapping our wings and squawking about the confines of the nest for several years now! Few of us anticipate anything but the excitement of freedom on the outside. Few expect the fear, the anxiety, the homesickness, the responsibility, and the loneliness that inevitably accompany our first solo flight.

Me, for one. I remember when, at the relatively advanced age of twenty, I stood on a train platform in my small Texas hometown on an Indian summer morning, feeling only the exhilaration of the journey ahead to a far northern college I had chosen for my graduate studies. That exhilaration stayed with me the entire trip as I talked and sang with the other students through the night, with scarcely a thought of what I'd left behind. And that, little did I suspect, was everything I ever knew or thought I knew about myself. Gone was that knowledge, that security of others knowing, acknowledging, accepting, loving that person that was me.

When the train pulled in at that unfamiliar Massachusetts station three days later, I stood dazed, amidst bags and footlockers galore, by the sudden realization that I was alone. I knew no one. But even worse, no one knew me. Feeling helpless and very much alone, I finally hailed a cab that deposited me, looking as if I'd just stepped out of *Vogue*, amidst a crowd of strangers in blue jeans at a very polished school. I grew quieter and quieter, trying desperately to hide my all too obvious uniqueness, my difference, my conspicuousness.

As I registered, and perfunctorily received my room assignment, the terrible truth began to dawn. For the first time in my life, I was going to have to stand up to all those strangers and say it: "This is who I am." Always before, people *knew* who I was! I had parents, grandparents, friends. No help from these staunch supporters now. No one to stand up and say, "Let me introduce this young lady out of *Vogue*."

There was nothing to do but gather up what seemed to be the totally inadequate pieces of myself—"gutting up," I now call it—and begin reaching out. Within three short weeks I had friends and acquaintances who recognized me, who acknowledged me, who saw me as whole. And, thanks to them, I was again.

It's a crucial time of development, this reaching out as an individual—standing up all alone sans all previous life-support systems. Some people never make it: the high school football star without his limelight, the beauty queen lost in a crowd of beauties, the valedictorian shuffled to the middle of the scholastic deck. These are the ones who always expect others to recognize them, to come to them. And when others don't, they may become disillusioned and bitter, shouting inside, "Don't they know who I *am?*" Sometimes, rather than take the initiative, these people turn back. You know the ones. They head for home—after a brief but respectable time at college or in the army or at a job in a different city—to the safety of the nest. Or they may choose to simply mark time, selling insurance or frozen yogurt and clinging close to familiar bars and faces, in their high school or college town long after graduation.

But for the majority of us who do make it—who do find the courage and the voice to stand up and say, "*This* is who *I* am. Who are *you?*"—it is a tremendously liberating experience. It's a gamble to be sure. And usually the winnings don't materialize overnight. It may take time and a lot of work. But to retreat, to bow out of the game, is a sure loss.

Kathy tells of her first year at a large university. Coming from a very status-conscious town, handicapped (or so she thought) by her lot as the daughter of parents who lived a bit too close to the railroad tracks, she found herself at last on her own, surrounded by interested, interesting people who wanted to know who she was. So she told them. And amazingly enough they were very much the same.

Friendships blossomed. Only occasionally was she reminded of her high school days, and then she easily laughed them off. She told me once of a time when a current young beau, a recent transfer from a prestigious eastern university, announced an impending visit from his fraternity brother and best friend, a young man named Thomas from her very high school. Quizzically, he asked Kathy if she were certain that she knew his friend, for when he had mentioned her, Thomas had replied, "Well, she must be a different girl from the one I knew." And she certainly was.

That break Kathy made, and in another sense received, freed her from what was past, from its constraints. These breaks, these opportunities, present themselves to all of us throughout our lives. But the *initial* break with all that is past—your home, your parents, some of your friends, and even your enemies —is one of the most important, for it marks the beginning of a continual learning process you will go through each time your world changes, each time you encounter something new and fresh whether that be a new city, a new job, or a new person.

It doesn't get much easier. Each time it takes the same type of "gutting up" it required of me that first day at the Massachusetts train station—that quiet time, that mustering of pieces of the self, that standing up and stepping forward to say, "This is me. Who are you?" With that first step, and with each one thereafter, we begin to trust ourselves and to realize that not only can we stand but we can walk, and not only walk but run as well.

The key is motion, movement, progression. It is this movement that gets us to our destination—to those different points in life we may reach, to those stations in those many cities each of us may visit. Some of us reach only one. Others reach them all. Where you stay, whom you meet, what you explore at each stop—all are unique. How you get from city to city is different. You may walk, crawl, dance, limp, run, or walk backward. Each of these ways is different in itself. But each involves movement, change, all the same. These changes are great in every decade of adult life. Beginning in our late teens, and about every ten years after that, we enter a critical period of transition—both individually and, as we will explore later, as a couple. These are periods of intense evaluation, when we examine the values, the "rules," that we have been developing since birth to guide our lives.

Now I said "examine," not discard. If we threw away all that we have been taught by our parents and society, it would create havoc. Eliminating all guidelines would force us to decide moment by moment how to relate and respond to others in our world, putting impossible demands on both time and energy. So inevitably we find that some of these values are good and helpful to us. Some require alteration. And some need to be thrown away. Each of these examination periods is a dynamic, often disruptive, time. It is a time of endings and beginnings; of doubts and decisions; and, consequently, of change. And much of it occurs in the decade between eighteen and twenty-eight. There are no sure bets before then, thank goodness.

Steve is living proof. At eighteen he was in total rebellion against his parents. He dropped out of high school and even served a jail sentence. Today, almost ten years later, he has a job he enjoys, owns his own home, and is a proud father. He assumes responsibility for himself with joy. Steve's changes were dramatic. He rejected all his parents' values, though they were healthy ones, and created a life-style that is totally his own—unique, different. It is one that both he and his parents can accept and respect despite their differences. This respect makes it possible for them to find new ways of relating to each other, to be friends.

Now suppose at eighteen we decide to stay home, or to marry and establish another home, without this parental break. We may stay the daughter or son for the rest of our lives, never quite cutting the proverbial apron strings. Unfortunately, these loose strings have a nasty way of tangling around our feet, making it difficult, if not impossible, to take those next necessary steps. They wrap around us in all sorts of ways, hampering movement and growth.

I'll never forget the forty-year-old woman I once counseled who was having difficulty understanding one of her teenagers. When I suggested that she might find some helpful insights in J. D. Salinger's *Catcher in the Rye*, I was promptly informed, in no uncertain terms, that she had no intention of reading such a book. "My mother," she stated flatly, "says it's an awful book. And my father always told me that you should respect the judgment of those you admire." I laughed, certain that she must be kidding, only to discover from her anger that I was sadly mistaken. Emotionally, I was dealing with a seventeen-year-old for whom this double parental bind was all too real.

This woman, with the apron itself draped over her head, is of course an extreme example. Usually the strings aren't quite so visible. But they cling to people like twenty-eight-year-old Ann—who explains in a little-girl voice that she wants to be cared for—and other women like her who remain "daddy's little girl," wanting to be taken care of, protected, told what to do. They curl around men like Drew, who remain "mother's boy," no matter how old they get.

Drew has always had people to take care of him and never learned to share responsibility. On his job he is very responsible. But at home he behaves like a little boy and expects his wife, Maria, to be both mother to and maid for him. Needless to say, this mother-son arrangement plays havoc with their relationship. Maria does not like being the mother to Drew but cannot find a way to stop. She sees him as a child, not a lover, and this oedipal twist of the apron strings creates a snarled knot in the bedroom.

At the opposite extreme we find the overly responsible men—and increasing numbers of women—who overreact to their need for a parent, for someone to care for them. These are the super independent, self-sufficient individuals who can do everything for themselves, who never need anyone. Jim, a respected physician, can do anything he sets his mind to. Married, with two children, he lives a loner's life. He does everything alone, although many avenues for sharing are open to him. He even develops elaborate systems to eliminate the need for help from others. For instance, rather than ask for help when he paved his driveway, he bought a wagon to haul the heavy cement. He does not see the sadness in his wife's eyes each time he insists, "I can do it myself." His fear of needing others, of being strangled by the ties, keeps her and others at arm's length.

Taking the shears to these strings is essential if we are ever to lay claim to our own lives, to give up the benefits of being the son or daughter so that we may become more completely ourselves. Sometimes drastic measures are required. Judy, a young working woman, told her loving but traditional mother and father that she was living with a man to determine whether or not they wanted to marry. Deeply hurt, her parents could not approve of this behavior and refused at first even to talk with the young man, Tom. Finally, after a year of sharing their lives and quarters, Judy and Tom were married in a quiet ceremony with only family and friends present. Her parents, ashamed of their daughter's previous living arrangements, could not bring themselves to host a reception until three months later. Today, after three years, Judy is expecting her first child. Her mother and father are the proud and joyous grandparents-to-be, now able to relate to her in the old, comfortable way, pretending their daughter has always been married.

The contrast is striking. Judy and Tom's marriage is based upon openness, caring, trust, and truth. They do not pretend. Pain and pretense, along with caring, form the underpinnings of Judy's parents' relationship. To insure that this was not her inheritance, Judy had to make the break. At first I thought she was wrong to tell her parents that she was living with Tom, for it is one thing to live your life as you wish but quite another to request the approval, or even understanding, of others. For Judy, however, the only weapon strong enough to get through the ties was the truth, all of it. Certainly there are other ways, but this one worked for her and, eventually, for her family.

It enabled her to stand alone, and this is essential before we can develop a complete relationship with another person. Without this separation, this aloneness, this distinction between "I" and "you," we cannot tell where we begin and others start. We are fused in. Sometimes this separation process is abrupt, as in Judy's case. Sometimes it is so gradual we are not even aware that it has happened.

Some people make this break at thirteen, some at twenty or thirty or sixty. Some never make it and are always limited in their relationships. They have never taken the time, or experienced the type of confrontation, that allows this growth. I have known some people who literally have never been alone, who went immediately from high school to college to marriage with no time or space to explore their own boundaries.

Always surrounded by others, they are afraid to be by themselves. This is extreme, to be sure, but it happens.

Don and Linda fall into this category. Although both are very dependent on one another, only Linda appears that way. Don is a civil engineer and Linda a bank officer who makes important business decisions every day. Yet in her relationship with Don, she is unable to decide even what she *thinks* without first checking it out with him. When she starts to voice an opinion, she turns to Don and watches his reaction to see if it's all right to proceed. She will literally ask, "Is that the way I feel?"

Don likes Linda's dependence on him in this way. It increases his sense of security, for he knows that she cannot leave him. He even states point blank that he does not want an independent wife but someone who defers to him as head of the household. They are like Siamese twins—fused. They cannot develop normally as adults because there is not enough room. There is no space to grow separately. When we do not feel that the other person is there, separate from us, we have to be constantly checking. This may actually work for a time. But problems arise if one person no longer wants this fused-in relationship but wants a sharing one instead, and the other does not change.

But creative solutions are possible. Diane and Jeff found one. They began as high school sweethearts in their small Georgia hometown. She, a perky, petite cheerleader and perfect student. He, an only child and an ambitious superachiever. They met when Diane was seventeen, Jeff, twenty, and married after her first year at college, when he had begun his MBA. Hard-driving, success-oriented, Jeff loved his wife and later his two daughters. But he wanted Diane to remain forever his little southern belle, whom he cared for and who, in return, thought of little else but the family. He was a benevolent dictator and she his willing slave.

The house was perfection, the children polished. There were well-balanced meals each evening, church on Sunday, and sex whenever Jeff was in the mood. But Diane managed these details of life quite mechanically, with no real sense of sharing with her husband.

Yet things went smoothly, until Jeff's job began to require a great deal of travel, and Diane was left to manage even more on her own. Feeling lonely and isolated, she turned to the man next door. With him she discovered that feelings were to be discussed, that sex was to be enjoyed, that she was to be seen and appreciated as an equal. She began to question what she was getting from Jeff in their marriage and even considered divorce. Jeff, however, could not understand. He wanted Diane to settle down, come to her senses, and get things back to status quo. So they separated, tacitly declaring their autonomy, their individuality.

Once they acknowledged, and assumed responsibility for, their separateness, Diane and Jeff began to change. Jeff began to want to feel close to Diane, to talk about feelings, to learn about sex, to share the responsibilities of parenthood. The separation lasted only six months. But today, three years later, they still keep a reminder of what it taught them—a key to the small apartment where Jeff lived during that time when they established the separateness they needed to feel truly married.

The process was indeed painful. There were years of anger, resentment, hate, and loneliness—a high price to pay for having skipped a few too many steps before they married. Retracing those steps was a slow, tedious, lonely process for both Diane and Jeff. But it was a necessary one that gave them, as two separate individuals, the courage to look honestly at the values, the rules, they had been living by; to change those that restricted; and to keep those that gave a sense of balance.

2

How You Got Here in the First Place

In shedding the roles, the masks, the illusions that confine our relationships, we discover the truth: There is no magic in this world, only make-believe. Contrary to our most fervent hopes, our most jealously guarded fantasies, love does not descend willy-nilly and whisk us away to live happily ever after. There is method to this divine madness, if we look close enough. There is a progression, a process.

As with any process, there is a starting point and a series of steps or stages leading to the final loving relationship we think of as marriage. Each step is distinct, yes. But all are continuous, essential components of the whole. Transitions to each stage are sometimes easy, sometimes difficult. But they are never automatic. And certainly they are not magical. It takes a desire to learn. It takes a willingness to work, to dig your heels in with each step and establish a foundation from which to move to the next.

The first step is the easiest, and the most mysterious. You are simply attracted to another person, drawn to him or her. And you step forward—right off the cliff.

ATTRACTION

Many a frustrated social scientist has tried to sort out the elements of attraction, but there is no clear-cut formula. Either it *is* or it *isn't*. Either you *are* or you *aren't*. Attraction, it seems, is a truly multidisciplinary event encompassing biology, chemistry, psychology, sociology, physiology, and more. Examining the myriad of unpredictable and downright astonishing matches people make, sorting out some common denominator appears, at first glance, to be a hopeless task. "I wonder what she sees in *him* [*her*]!" we catch ourselves thinking, trying to solve this apparently insolvable puzzle. The couple I spotted dining at a nearby table recently underscored the mystery. Strangers to me, they commanded my attention. The woman, somewhere in her fifties, was starkly unadorned: no makeup, too closely cropped hair, and at least forty pounds overweight. The man appeared to be ten years younger: trim, elegantly attired, hair a perfect silver gray. Yet when he looked at his partner, contentedly and lovingly touched her arm, the spark —the attraction—was unmistakable. Together they selected a wine, and he offered a toast to the warm, beautiful woman he saw sharing his table.

Something was there, all right. But I could not perceive it. Certainly, each individual's definition of an "attractive" partner is different. Yet in observing hundreds of couples, I have discovered a common ingredient, a single quality, that draws one person to another. I call it vitality. Each of us is attracted to those individuals who appear, to *us*, to have this vitality—who are full of life and vigor, who have a capacity for developing and living life to its fullest.

Each of us has his or her own definition of this vitality. Think for a minute of the people you are attracted to, regardless of age or sex. You may find them intelligent, athletic, gregarious, reserved, artistic, ambitious, successful, or sensitive. Undoubtedly, you will discover a common "mix" of attributes that you find engaging and attractive about them.

Fortunately, the right mix is different for each person. So in the potpourri of humanity, there's usually something for everyone. That mix, that particular configuration of characteristics that draws us to another person, has everything to do with our own personal mix—our needs, our strengths, our limitations, and, perhaps most important, our perceptions. For it is on our perceptions, and *ours* alone, that attraction hinges.

But appearances can be deceiving. Our senses often play tricks on us. And we see what we want to see. Like many women, Kay always found herself attracted to the strong, silent man, a man of action rather than talk. Phil was such a man: tall, blond, athletic, quiet. But beneath that cool exterior, Kay perceived (or so she thought) a great deal of vitality. Like her, Phil was action-oriented, enjoying tennis, skiing, and camping. Kay wanted to share these activities. So she married Phil, only to discover that he liked sharing them with men only. Phil, on the other hand, wanted a woman who took care of herself and pursued her own interests, independent of him. Kay looked like the ticket. Little did he know that she wanted to share in his activities and in his feelings. Little did she know that he had nothing, beyond that cool, quiet exterior, to share.

Beth, in contrast, was attracted to the sensitive charmers like Kevin. Dashing and romantic, Kevin knew all the tricks to turn a woman's head. On their first date he presented Beth with a single red rose, which she carried on their moonlit walk along the beach. She was convinced that Kevin was the most stimulating, vital, alive man she had ever known. But the magic ended when Beth discovered that Kevin's romantic moods alternated, at about three-week intervals, with serious bouts of depression, which put an intolerable burden on their relationship.

Kay and Beth were both irresistibly drawn to men whom they perceived to be more vital and alive than themselves. These were people whom they perceived had something to give, to offer, to share. Just what that is, or as Kay and Beth found out *isn't*, requires that we scratch below that oh-so-attractive surface and probe for something more substantial upon which we can build. This probing process goes both ways. It involves a give-and-take between two people. It involves interaction. It involves sharing.

SHARING

Through sharing we begin to search for something more to see if, in fact, this attractive individual really has everything he or she seems to have, and at least a few of the things we need. It is through this sharing process that the relationship begins to move forward or comes to a screeching halt. It starts small, sharing activities, time, friends, and feelings on a beginning level. And it starts early, filling up the silence and the "space" between two people with conversation and activity. If it's not there, few people can endure the awkward silences or empty spaces for long. It's uncomfortable and, worse yet, *boring*. You can tell when it's missing. Look around a crowded restaurant some evening and see if you can't spot it—the silent couples, concentrating on the pizza supreme or chicken kiev: hesitant, awkward, eager couples on their first date; resigned, tired, bored couples who have been married two or ten or twenty years. The former are hopeful, the latter tragic. But the missing element is the same. There is no interchange, no sharing.

Early in a relationship, we play it safe, sharing only those things on the periphery of ourselves. But it marks the beginning, that step forward to say, "This is who I am. Who are you?" It is by sharing experiences together that we begin to develop a relationship or to see if one can be developed. This is true of all relationships. Through sharing even simple tasks— with neighbors, co-workers, friends of friends—we begin to see if a relationship can develop and is worth developing. It is a way of reaching out and establishing a common ground upon which to build a more substantial relationship: friend, colleague, confidant, lover. It is a starting point. It is why people join together with others to square dance or ski or to play bridge or racquetball. They not only want to learn and enjoy an activity but also to share with others while doing it.

It is through sharing that we develop relationships. As we build through sharing the little things, we are able to share the big ones: our dreams and our disappointments, as well as the details of our lives. But the little things provide the basis for continued sharing throughout the development of the relationship. Day-to-day sharing of activities and interests is essential in establishing and maintaining a couple's feeling of closeness. Cooperation and a fair share of compromise are musts if these shared activities are to get beyond that lowest common denominator: the TV set! Two people invariably have different interests. And finding ways to share them often requires a little imagination, if not outright determination.

Art was an avid tennis player, spending two afternoons a week on the courts while Sheila tapped her foot impatiently, awaiting his arrival home and feeling cheated, left out, separate. "But you're a terrible tennis player," Art whined. Undaunted, Sheila took tennis lessons. She was still pretty terrible but accomplished enough to play a fumbling match with the equally left-out wife of Art's favorite partner. So two afternoons a week there is a foursome—the two men volleying on one court, the two women chasing balls on the next. The foursome shares not just a tennis court but time and company and themselves.

Even sharing household chores can go a long way toward increasing the closeness between two people. Now, I'm not talking about a fifty-fifty division of labor but true sharing. After five years together Connie and David now laugh about their early efforts in this department. Connie is one of those people who is blissfully oblivious to her surroundings, sidestepping mundane housekeeping details at every possible opportunity. Before she moved in with David, she had perfected all sorts of ingenious ways to economize on the time devoted to such chores. Washing dishes is a good example. Leaving dirty dishes in the sink was an open invitation to resident roaches. So Connie neatly stacked them in her sparsely stocked refrigerator until the supply in the cabinet ran dangerously low. But surroundings were important to David, and Connie knew it. So before they took up residence together, they made a fifty-fifty bargain where housekeeping chores were concerned. Within a month, Connie realized her folly, wailing, "Half of what *David* wants done is *twice* as much as I would do on my own!"

Taken issue by issue, this often looks trivial and seems silly to argue about. "Put your dirty dishes in the dishwasher or the roaches will have a feast," or "Clean the tub when you get out or the hair will clog the drain." But David didn't think that they were trivial as he pointedly scoured the shower each week. And neither did Connie as she grudgingly shouldered David's definition of "50 percent." The problems appear deceptively easy to solve. Each person just takes the responsibility to clean the tub after a shower or to put the dishes away. Yet, when we resolve one problem, we often find, like the sorcerer's apprentice, that ten more spring up to take its place. Addressing the issue problem by problem does not work, for it is a *process*—not any given task or activity—that is the sharing. It applies as well to cleaning the tub as to taking the initiative in lovemaking. It's not something you can divide and assign fifty-fifty. And it doesn't lend itself to scorekeeping.

This is a difficult concept to understand in our society. For the last thirty years, we have been taught to divide the responsibilities, not to share them. Sometimes this division is necessary. For example, when a father works outside the home, the mother may assume responsibility for that full-time, equally demanding job known as homemaking. But finances, the rearing of children, and the care of the home on weekends should be a shared responsibility, not one to be divided equally. This sharing is what enables a relationship to grow. If mother and father share equally in child rearing, for instance, the benefits are twofold: Both parents increase their sense of closeness to one another, and they increase that closeness with the children. As more and more couples experiment with this sharing process, they reap some surprising benefits. Men are coming to know their children and their wives. Women are becoming more a part of, not servant to, their families.

It's a feeling of doing, being together. It is only when that feeling is not there that we get out the scorecards. Then the trivial becomes the monumental. We confuse the problems with the process, and the problems become the pivot points for bitter struggles.

Drew and Maria, whom we met earlier, have been married less than a year but are in constant conflict because they cannot share. The household chores are a good example. Maria would become livid over the fact that the lawn (*his* job!) went untended for two weeks, pitting her fury against this trivial problem instead of the real issue that she had gone unloved in the bedroom even longer. As intimacy and sex waned, Maria sought to increase her sense of security or control by demanding that Drew "do his duty" around the house, if not in the bedroom. That put her in charge, directing the show, making it impossible to share. When we truly share, no one is in charge. We work together to get things done.

For some of us, this sharing comes easily because we were raised in an environment where sharing was fun. But for some of us—like Diane and Jeff—it is a painstaking process because we have never really learned what sharing means. Diane and her sister never learned to share in a positive way. Each week their father gave each girl a separate list of household duties. Then every Saturday he conducted an inspection of completed chores. This arrangement threw the two girls into direct competition with each other for their father's favor. Neither learned the fun of sharing. Instead each saw the other as a competitor rather than a partner. Jeff, too, was denied true sharing experiences. He was an only child, whose doting parents and relatives catered to his every whim. Jeff's wishes were the order of the day. And asking Jeff to help or share in any household chores or activities was unthinkable.

Because neither Jeff nor Diane knew the first thing about sharing when they married, neither could teach the other about this crucial process. In fact, neither was even aware that such a feeling of sharing existed, having never experienced it. Diane was used to orders, and Jeff certainly knew how to give them. They could not even share the simple tasks of life, much less the big ones.

But Diane got an inkling of what it felt like to share during her brief affair. And it felt good. Admitting first that neither knew how to get and keep this feeling together, Diane and Jeff began to learn. They started by sharing a simple activity—backpacking. At first, Jeff forged ahead with the boys and Diane followed behind. Then she convinced him that it would be much more fun if they all hiked together. So they did. And it was. Today Diane and Jeff share the adventure of weekend hikes or week-long treks through mountains or piney woods.

Certainly, I do not mean to imply that couples must do everything together. We must move apart and come back together so that each partner receives input from a variety of sources. This flux enables each to bring something to the relationship. Without it couples become Siamese twins. But I do mean that sharing requires that we do enough real, literal sharing together to build to the next stage of the relationship: caring.

CARING

Caring is a process that encompasses, but goes beyond, sharing. It involves, more than anything, wanting. Wanting to be with the person you care for. Wanting to know how he or she feels; wanting that person to know how you feel. Wanting to see and understand; wanting to be seen and understood. But this wanting goes hand in hand with a willingness to invest, to give, what you yourself most need to receive. Caring, then, in one sense, is a deepening of sharing. It involves more than sharing words, activities, time. It involves sharing feelings. And that makes it a dynamic process.

I can talk for hours with my friend Carol about how we feel about a book we have read and, more than that, how we feel about those feelings. Our conversation becomes far more than a dry discussion of a book. This is the kind of sharing that brings people close, that adds vitality to relationships. Without it we dry up inside. It's tiring, even exhausting, to simply talk about "things" rather than our feelings about them. Life becomes one giant cocktail party where you discuss all sorts of "things"—the weather, problems with the children, the latest movies. With that kind of stimulation, who needs sleeping pills?

Many people have never experienced true caring, this feeling of being close to another person. When I first tried to describe it to Gary, his expression told me I might just as well have been speaking Greek. Gary had been married to Jean for twenty-five years when he first came into therapy. An intelligent man with a Ph.D. in biochemistry under his belt, Gary had literally no concept of how to be close to someone. Jean had resigned herself to being married, but alone, until she discovered Gary's three-year affair. Although she was hurt by his infidelity, that was not the real issue. Jean's fury sprang from the apparent fact that, contrary to everything she had experienced, Gary *could* be involved with someone. Now she demanded equal rights.

But Gary had no idea of how to be close and loving. In truth, his relationship with his ex-mistress had not progressed beyond the attraction stage. He could not understand what Jean meant by being "open," by sharing and talking about his feelings. Suffering the universal pain of having feelings rebuffed and misunderstood as an adolescent, Gary literally decided that he would not let anyone know how he felt. It could hurt. When he realized that being close or intimate required that he *talk* about feelings, he put his foot down. And so did Jean. Either he talk, she demanded, or she was leaving.

He decided to start talking. With Gary, as with most

of us, it took a crisis to stimulate change. Only the threat of losing Jean was enough to give him the courage to risk being more open and caring in their relationship. Change is often frightening. And only when faced with losing what we have, or changing, will we take the gamble and begin the hard work necessary to keep and sustain what is valuable to us. This is the type of confrontation that we think of as a crisis point in the development of a relationship.

Gary first had to realize and accept that this kind of sharing does not come easily. We must cultivate the closeness. Usually it is the man who does not understand this type of closeness, or the need for it. In fact, it looks like a flagrant violation of one of those nasty little rules we inherited: Never trust a woman. Literature, social mores, and cultural attitudes all perpetuate the view of women as the "intimate enemy," not to be trusted with the feelings of a man. They gossip and divulge secrets. Any disclosure of tender or vulnerable feelings to such creatures is a direct breach of personal security. They are threatening. And when we feel threatened, we close down. We pull back into our shells, rather than stick our necks out further. Ironically, however, the ultimate threat to security, as in Gary's case, is the threat of desertion, of loneliness, of total loss. Only when Jean announced, "I'm leaving," could Gary muster the courage to do whatever it took to preserve the security that Jean's caring gave him. That meant sticking his neck out—all the way out— only to find that the old rules didn't apply. Jean could be trusted with his feelings. She cared for him even more. And in that caring, he could feel secure.

Certainly, this is not to say that this problem is common to, nor limited to, the male of the species. In fact, oddly enough, there's a similar rule still on the books for women: You just can't trust a man. And a lot of women buy it. What is important is that the partner who does recognize this need for closeness and openness be committed to helping the other person reach out to meet it.

For Gary, this reaching out began in desperation. But begin it did, with the admission that he was not open and caring in his relationship with Jean. From this point, he could begin, at first mechanically and then spontaneously, to reach out; to acknowledge his caring for Jean; and, more importantly, to reveal that caring to her openly. For instance, although he was frequently late in getting home from work, Gary never telephoned Jean to offer any explanation. To him, this kind of "reporting in" behavior was asking, like a child, for Jean's permission to be late. He saw her demands that he call just to say, "I'm running a couple of hours behind schedule," as an effort to control him, rather than a caring act stemming from her worry and concern for him. During this crisis period, Gary decided to take a chance. He called Jean one evening just to say, "I'll be a couple of hours late." Her warm response, rather than anger at his delay, encouraged him and made him feel cared for. Jean, too, felt cared about, knowing that Gary thought enough of their relationship to call. Small successes like this one prompted Gary to share more of himself with Jean—his feelings about work, about her. That gave Jean something, *someone*, to respond to in an equally caring way. The payoff for both of them set up a positive spiral—care and be cared for—instead of a downward spin. It is the momentum of this caring process that encourages both Gary and Jean to be more open and caring in their relationship.

This openness between two people, this closeness, provides a common ground where each literally shares the other's feelings about something. It enables us to share those parts of ourselves, those experiences we have, that are separate from the other person. This is the type of sharing that brings two lives into the relationship. It is what makes it possible to share a sunrise seen, a baby's first step, or a personal achievement with a partner. Although it's not the same as sharing together, we can tell the other person what we have seen or done, and that person can experience it in the same way we did.

Sometimes it is joy we share. Amy told her husband of the hawk she sometimes saw soaring on the wind from their back porch, and of the sense of freedom he brought her. They lived in a heavily populated suburban area, so the hawk did not come often. But one spring day Peter ran into the kitchen shouting to Amy to come outside. From the urgency in his voice, she feared one of the children was hurt. But when she reached him, he took her hand and said, "Look, there is our hawk, our sign for a good day together."

Sometimes, too, it is pain we must share. Joe came home one day to find Glenda in tears. Her best friend's husband had been transferred, and they were moving to another state. Joe didn't try to cheer Glenda by saying, "For goodness' sakes, we'll be seeing them next month on vacation, and besides, you can always call her." Instead, he took her in his arms and said, "Go ahead and cry. We don't lose good friends every day."

These small joys and pains are the very foundation of a relationship. It is the sharing of these kinds of feelings that enables us to build the trust to share more and more of ourselves, both with our partner and with others. It also brings us a sense of closeness, a sense of not being alone in our joy or pain. Both experiences are enhanced by sharing.

This type of vicarious sharing comes, again, from wanting—wanting to know what the other person has seen and done, wanting to be with that person in this way. We do not literally have to be there to share. We only have to want to know what happened to the other person to share that experience. However, this type of sharing is impossible unless there are moments each day in which we share experiences together, building the reservoir of feelings of closeness that only literal sharing can produce.

This sharing on all levels and the openness and caring that make it possible provide the footholds by which we move to the next stage of the relationship: intimacy. It's dangerous territory. But the mutual trust we have built by this point gives us the security of knowing that one slipup isn't the end. And that gives us the courage to move forward.

INTIMACY

The transition to this level in a relationship can occur at any time. Some couples reach this stage within weeks in a relationship. Others never reach it in thirty years of marriage. It is in this stage that into the mix of attraction, sharing, and caring, we stir a measure—large or small—of intensity. It is intensity that heightens our awareness of the other person. We become acutely aware of his or her needs, wants, and desires, as well as of our own. And we want and need to express and share them.

This intensity stems, once again, from a deep-seated need, a wanting. Wanting to be with the other person more than anyone else. Wanting to share spontaneously without worry of acceptance. Wanting to share the joy of an experience with the other person, both physically and verbally. Wanting to help when the other person is hurt or in pain. Wanting to talk about, express our feelings about, the relationship and wanting to work to improve it.

The degree of this intensity in a relationship, as in any activity, is directly proportional to how much we want it and are willing to work for it. For example, I may want to play the guitar. How much I want it is directly related, say on a scale of 1 to 10, to how well I will play. If I simply talk about how much I want to play but never even bother to take lessons, I rate about a 1 on this "wanting" scale. If I take lessons every Tuesday but do not practice in between, I tip the scale at 2. I don't want enough to expend a great deal of effort. If I practice occasionally, I might rate a 3 or 4. Now if I want to play the guitar so much that not only do I take lessons but I also practice faithfully every day, I'd rate a 5. The more I practice, the better I play. The better I play, the more I enjoy it. The more I enjoy it, the more I play—that is, *practice.* Before I know it, the work (the practice) *becomes* the pleasure (playing), and the process spurs me into the 6–10 range on the wanting scale. At this level, I have the basics. I will travel up and down on this end of the scale, depending on how much I want, and feel like investing, at any point in time. On the weeks I don't want much and don't practice much, I may slide back to 6. But the next week, I may play daily, enjoy playing daily, and want to play on level 9. So I'll work toward it. And I'll get there, if I want it badly enough.

The same is true in a relationship. Many couples have told me, "We want to work on our relationship." Some simply come and sit in my office together once a week and do nothing, practice nothing, in between sessions. Not surprisingly, nothing very much happens in their relationship. Others do their homework. They literally work at home, spending, at my instruction, a specified amount of time each week talking with each other about their feelings. At first they complain, "But it's so mechanical!" And I agree that it is, for they are working to acquire the basic skills they need to make this practice *pleasure.* Within two weeks most begin to feel less mechanical and find themselves "practicing" far more than the required time because they *enjoy* it. It increases their sense of closeness to one another. It heightens the degree of intensity—and, hence, intimacy—between them. They have the basics and are ready to explore the 6–10 range of their wanting scale. And, as with my guitar playing, their degree of pleasure—of closeness, of intimacy—will ebb and flow in direct proportion to their wanting, and their willingness to work for it.

This degree of intimacy remains in flux, constantly changing as the people within the relationship change. Depending on individual wants and needs at different times in the relationship, couples move from closeness to distance to isolation, and back to closeness again. In their late twenties, as the man and/or woman progresses rapidly up the career ladder with small children in tow, closeness usually suffers. Couples will move very close together again in their thirties when they quit fighting jobs and preschoolers, only to pull apart around forty, and become close again as they approach fifty. These ten-year swings are not only common but *normal*. They are to be expected, accepted, and moved with.

Yet even in the midst of the closest, most intense periods, individuals need a sense of space, of coming together and moving away. It is this flow that gives the feeling of love a chance to be with us without overwhelming us. Lisa and Frank can spend a peaceful day on their sailboat, feeling intensely close. They touch and talk, then sit quietly and introspectively, only to move back to touching and conversation. If they spent the whole day together talking and touching nonstop, they would be exhausted. Instead they return to shore feeling refreshed and warm—and closer to each other.

Many people say they want this type of intimate relationship but will find all sorts of excuses not to put out the effort required: "We would do it if we had more time," or, "If only the job [or the kids, or the house] weren't so demanding." These couples hold their relationship at 2, pretending that it is the external forces that keep them apart rather than their internal refusal to risk working for a more intimate relationship. Their investment is small, and so are their dividends. In contrast, some couples, like Margaret and Bill, go for broke.

After eighteen years of marriage, Margaret had given up on trying to be close to Bill. So she had turned to other relationships—her six children, her friends, her community—to satisfy her need for closeness. Bill, on the other hand, found satisfaction through his work and the women with whom he had occasional and delicately concealed affairs. Margaret and Bill had developed a model partnership as both parents and community leaders. But Margaret felt cheated, cut off from Bill and the intimacy she wanted (on at least an 8 level!) in their relationship. So she began to try again to get closer to her husband. When she got close enough to discover Bill's current paramour, she demanded a divorce.

Looking at the stakes—eighteen years of sharing with and caring for, if not feeling particularly close to, Margaret versus a few months with the other woman —Bill terminated the affair. By this time, Margaret and Bill had only two options: to work toward a more fulfilling, intimate relationship or to divorce. Win, lose, but no draw.

It took them a year to learn even the basic skills for developing an intimate relationship, to nudge up to 6 on the scale. One night they made a real breakthrough. Bill, torn between his wanting to be close and his fear of being close, shook Margaret awake at two in the morning just to talk. And for the first time, she felt, "He wants to be as close as I do." The wanting was there. The work was yet to come. It was not easy, and not always pleasant.

Bill and Margaret ruined many an expensive dinner because the working required conflict. One of the many times they were trying to feel close, they went to their favorite restaurant for dinner, hoping that might help. Over hors d'oeuvres, Margaret began to tell Bill how lonely she had been, feeling that he had not taken the time to be with her lately. Bill tried to pacify her with, "You know how much work I've had at the office this week." The fight escalated from there. "The kids have had the flu all week, but I've made time for you," Margaret whispered through clenched teeth. "Your work is no excuse!" They left their meal untouched and stormed to the car. But instead of heading straight home, they drove around until they both understood the other's wants and feelings.

Today Margaret and Bill have what they wanted. They have that close, intimate relationship. And they achieved it under very trying circumstances. Between the demands on Bill's time at the office and six children between the ages of two and sixteen, they managed to find time to work, to practice, three times a week at communicating honestly with each other.

This *honest* communication of what you want—of your attraction, your caring, your desire to share— is the cornerstone of intimacy. But it is not as easy as it sounds. Although Tony and Suzanne had never been close to each other in fifteen years of marriage, Tony knew what he wanted. "I just want her to put her arms around me and say 'I love you. Let's be friends,'" he told me. "I need her to like and want me as I like and want her."

But he was afraid to ask for what he wanted. So he tried the indirect route. "Let's fly to the Ozarks and go fishing. It's beautiful there," Tony would say, then launch into a long dissertation about a new type of lure the fish would find irresistible. "No thanks," Suzanne would respond. "I don't want to go fishing. I'll stay here. Why don't you take Terry [their oldest boy]? He likes to fish!"

When Tony learned to tell Suzanne what he really wanted, the invitation came out, "I want to go away with you, just the two of us. I want to have a chance to really be together without the pressure of the job and the kids around. I want to share that with you. I want to be close to you." Astonished, Suzanne's answer was, "Oh, my! What a *wonderful* idea!" For years, they had missed the pleasure and fulfillment that this intimacy can provide because neither could express the feeling simply, directly, honestly: "I want to be close to you."

This wanting, this acknowledgment of our need for closeness, is the first step. Practice is the second. It is through the development and polishing of these skills—the sharing, the caring, the intimacy—that a relationship develops the depth that leads to commitment.

COMMITMENT

This commitment, contrary to popular belief, is not a one-shot, all-or-nothing decision. It is for today only, not forever. Yet when I say, "I am committed for this day," many people become alarmed, even angry. They feel that this is not commitment, that it has to be a life sentence! They feel that a person is committed only if he or she says, "I'll love you forever." They believe this pledge carries permanence. The divorce statistics prove otherwise. This kind of commitment is impossible to make. Certainly, we can pledge to be married and physically stay with someone throughout our lifetime. But to love, and emotionally be with them forever, no.

We can say, "I'll try to love you each day and work at it." But we cannot promise to love someone forever, for life is constantly changing. If a couple promises to try to love each other, their relationship has a chance to be dynamic, vital, and growing—not one they cannot afford to examine too closely or one that must be protected from harsh truths or taken for granted.

How many marriages are ruined because couples cannot look honestly at how they feel about each other each and every day? I suspect that over half suffer from this neglect. Yet individuals in the singles groups I address become most upset by the motto I Am Committed for Today. Many are divorced. They have been hurt. And they want a guarantee that someone will love them forever the second time around—not so that life will be alive and fulfilling but so that they will be safe. We cheat ourselves by this attitude throughout life. We are afraid to risk. We are afraid to become involved.

By playing it safe, we shut down the growth of a relationship. We sacrifice the involvement—the sharing, the caring, the intimacy—that is the critical dimension of true commitment. We can be committed in a relationship but not involved. Not sharing. Not caring. Not intimate. But we cannot be involved without being committed. I have seen people who have been committed to a marriage for thirty years but have never been involved with their spouse. But I have never seen anyone who is involved with someone who is not committed. So in looking at the ingredients, the building blocks of a relationship, we have to look at not only commitment but the degree of involvement.

"I can't wait to tell him what happened today! He will want to know how I feel." This is involvement—

knowing, "He will care about me. And I will care about him." Sounds simple. But as with all the other essential ingredients of relating we've been discussing, the process takes a lot of work. It takes first wanting to tell our partner what happened and how we feel about it. It takes sorting out our feelings and trusting that the other person will want to share them. And it takes listening—on both sides.

To listen, not just pretend to listen, requires that we not only hear the words but search for what is behind them. When we're really listening, we want to ask questions about what we've heard, about the details of what has happened, about our partner's feelings about those happenings. And we want to remember what the other person tells us because it is important, to that person and to us.

Sally didn't feel it was important to Ray. In many a posh or plain restaurant, she vied with strangers for his attention. As she tried to share her thoughts and feelings with him, he tried to pretend he was listening. But his attention wandered to the door each time a new diner arrived. In their seven years of marriage, Sally had repeatedly explained to Ray that she needed him to talk to her, to listen to her, to be involved with her. And she didn't feel this involvement when his interest shifted to the restaurant door each time a new face appeared. Ray's answer was always, "I'm listening. I can do two things at once." Yet he never talked about his feelings or asked Sally questions about hers.

One evening, after another futile monologue, Sally rose from the table saying, "Excuse me, Ray. I'll be right back." Feigning a trip to the powder room, she exited through the back door of the restaurant, walked around to the front, and entered. When Ray looked up to see who was coming in, she smiled and waved. Ray began to get the message. He began to listen. They began to talk and become involved with one another.

This involvement may simply mean asking "How was your day?" and really wanting an answer! With that question, we're asking our partner for more than "What did you do today?" We're asking about him or her, what he or she experienced, how he or she felt about it. We're not asking for a minute-by-minute account of activities but how our partner *felt* about those activities. Lisa, for instance, certainly has no interest in the intricacies of a functioning, or nonfunctioning, distributor. But her partner, Frank, finds them fascinating. And she finds him fascinating. So she is interested, not in rebuilding a distributor but in how Frank *feels* about rebuilding a distributor— how he feels defeated in trying to complete the job and how satisfied and excited he feels when it works. We don't want the facts, really. We want the feelings, *really!* We want to be involved with the other person and his or her life. We want to share with that person and care for him or her when we're involved. If we're committed only, we simply want to show a wedding ring.

Yet what is it that spurs us toward involvement and commitment? What makes us feel all the wanting that impels us to move through all these stages? After all, it's a lot of trouble! It is our basic human need, our hunger, for love.

LOVE

I'm not sure what love is exactly. Love has been defined by all kinds of people: poets, songwriters, theologians, therapists. But it hasn't been defined in a way I can accept, describe, and feel I know as I do all the other steps. Sex, certainly, is not love. Sex, in fact, can be a part of any level of the relationship. It does not require anything past attraction to occur. It may not even require that. Nor is being "in love" the same as love. Being in love comes only in attraction and sharing. It does not encompass the stages of caring and intimacy. Being in love often brings a feeling of intimacy or involvement. But you cannot truly care for the other person because you cannot see or perceive him or her clearly.

Love may come as part of sharing, part of caring, part of intimacy. I must say that each of these is a part of loving someone. And then again, I must say that you can do and feel all these things and still not experience the kind of love necessary for a marriage relationship. People feel this way with close friends, up to and including intimacy. And yet I know couples who are not doing, feeling, half of what I have described who truly love each other. Love is therefore all of this, part of this, but more. It is the ingredient that determines whether or not a marriage is satisfying and to what degree.

A professor I once had said, "Many things cause negative change in a person. But only three things can cause positive change: a truly religious experience, psychotherapy, and love." All these forces work on the inner core of a person, that part of us that must be affirmed as special and unique. They all require that we quit using words to describe others, that we experience and relate to others as individuals.

I have seen people who have had a truly religious experience transformed from unhappy, introverted people who could see only themselves into outgoing, warm, caring individuals. I once witnessed this kind of transformation in a man who was notorious for his shady business deals and ill-concealed affairs. Hoping to make some new sales contacts, he quite by accident attended a Christian businessmen's meeting one weekend. He returned on Monday a changed man. He became a pillar of the community, devoting his time and energy to helping those around him. He committed himself to his marriage, and he and his wife built a whole new world together. Eight years later, he is still a man of honor and integrity in all his relationships: business, community, and marriage.

I have also seen people so caught up in their neuroses that they could not be intimate with anyone. After therapy they are able to reach out and become truly involved for the first time. Roger, for instance, had never been close to anyone—mother, father, brothers, friends, or his wife of thirteen years. He could experience his wife's caring for him but could not feel the need to be close, to be intimate. As he became aware of this inability to feel close, he began the process of learning what intimacy and love are all about. It was a slow process because he had none of the tools to work with. Teaching a thirty-year-old adult how to be intimate is like teaching a thirty-year-old how to read. It requires adding one skill to another—sharing, caring—in a building way. It takes daily practice and work. Roger has begun this process, and he knows it will be slow. His awareness of self and others continues to expand each day. It is like opening up a whole new world for him, one that he never knew existed so was unable to work toward.

And every once in a while, I have seen people really loved who can then turn to others in a loving way. Dennis is one. He quit college after his sophomore year because he felt isolated, depressed, lonely. In his early thirties, he worked as an assistant manager at a small local radio station, where his contact with other people was minimal. He never dated. By this time he had progressed from overweight to obesity and was hospitalized for high blood pressure. During his stay a young nurse initiated a friendship by inviting him to her home for dinner. That was the beginning. She developed a love for him that was totally accepting and caring. He accepted that love, lost weight, and returned to school to earn a doctorate in art history. He emerged as a person who could care for others and reach out in a loving way.

Loving someone, as the nurse did Dennis, is a feeling we express through our doing with, sharing with, and caring for one another. We may do many things for many people, yet not love them. So doing, alone, is not loving.

In *Fiddler on the Roof* the dairyman asks his wife of many years, "Do you love me?" She reminds him, "I've washed your clothes, cooked your meals. . . ." "But do you love me?" he persists. ". . . given you children," she dodges. "But do you love me? Do you love me?" he cajoles. She replies "I suppose I do." The loving is a feeling we have that gives the doing, the act, meaning and purpose. Not just washing your clothes but caring for you. Not just raising the children but sharing with you. Doing in a loving way.

The perfect housewife may not be at all loving. She may keep an immaculate house in response to her own compulsive needs, not out of love. Similarly, a man may say, "I work hard to earn a living for you. I must love you." Not so. People work for themselves, not for someone else. Pure and simple.

Loving acts are not thinly disguised acts of self-sacrifice. They are, instead, acts of self-fulfillment. To act in a loving way, you must first *feel* loving. Second, you must go to the trouble of finding out how to express this loving feeling to your partner in a way he or she can experience it as loving. Our objective is to express our love and to find fulfillment in both that expression and in our partner's response.

In self-sacrifice, however, our objective is completely different. First, we do not *feel* loving but want to be perceived by our partner as loving. Second, we go only to the trouble of deciding how to best manipulate our partner into feeling that we have sacrificed—and that now he or she owes *us* something.

Martha felt this sense of indebtedness when she opened a box containing a much too expensive Christmas fur coat from her husband, Alex. She knew that they were in debt up to their ears, so she felt that Alex must really love her to have bought the coat. But she didn't feel loved, exactly. She felt guilty. She felt guilty because she really didn't like fur coats. She felt guilty because Alex had spent money on her that they did not have. And she felt even guiltier when Alex confided in her that he had foregone attending an important professional conference to buy the coat. In contrast, Alex felt smug and self-sacrificing. Neither he nor Martha felt anything even remotely related to love. So there was no sense of self-fulfillment on either side.

In this case neither the feeling nor its expression was right. Sometimes the feeling can be there but the expression of it wrong. You feel loving toward your partner but fail to get your message across.

Nancy approached her fortieth birthday with great anticipation. It was a very special day for her, a milestone. So her husband, Hal, wanted to give her something extra special—something that said "I love you." Knowing how badly Nancy needed the faulty air conditioning in her car fixed, he decided that this would be the most loving gift he could give her. He labored over the car for days with a real feeling of love and then presented Nancy with his handiwork the day before her birthday. Her response was something less than overwhelming.

The next day, Nancy began dressing early for the extra special birthday dinner she felt certain Hal had planned for her. But when she greeted him at the door, he asked, astonished, "Why are you all dressed up? Where are we going?" She burst into tears before she could even blurt out, "It's my birthday!"

What went wrong? Hal felt loving, so that went right. But he did not know how to express that feeling for Nancy in a way she could experience as love. That's what went wrong. But, in all fairness, I should point out that Nancy did not tell Hal that what she wanted most were flowers and a special dinner. Without that information he could not understand her needs. Believe me, she told him that night.

On her forty-first birthday Hal greeted Nancy at the door with at least a dozen bouquets. And her special dinner arrived by caterer. Hal felt the same love he did the year before. But this time Nancy experienced the love, for he expressed it in a way that she could understand.

Many people think I am asking them to be false when I say, "Find out what makes your partner feel loved. Then do it!" But certainly it is not false or self-sacrificing to feel love and want to express it. Certainly it is not false to want to get the message across when you feel it, in a way the other person can understand. If the act is based on real feeling, simply changing its expression is not false. It is only false when there is no feeling.

This feeling, this loving, is what marriage is all about. There is a quality about it that is undefinable, yet unmistakable. And it expresses itself in many ways: in acceptance, in trust, in intensity.

Leslie laughs as she describes her husband: "Eric scares people off because he appears so hard and gruff out front. His bark is so loud that people never find out what a pushover he is." "He's so sensitive, he cries if one of us gets hurt," their sixteen-year-old daughter echoes. "But he acts to the world like nothing could affect him."

What they say is very true. A hulk of a man, Eric

stands over six feet four inches and tips the scale at 240 pounds. When you first meet him, his face seems closed, often frowning. But when he becomes comfortable enough to relax in your company, he is like a big lovable dog who wants nothing more than to please and be close to you. Leslie sees and accepts this shyness, not as something to hold against Eric or criticize him for but as a part of the person she loves.

Liz is just the opposite. While her husband, Andy, sees her faults, he accepts them and loves her in a way one usually sees only in very young marriages. "I wouldn't change anything about Liz," he says, "except her undying efforts to change me!"

Liz, on the other hand, is constantly correcting Andy —after thirty-two years of marriage, in which he has always built her up, laughed in a loving way at her limitations. She, in turn, belittles him, criticizes his shortcomings, refuses to accept his limitations. While Liz is able to be loving toward the children, in her relationship with Andy, she becomes unloving and at times even cruel. She feels that unless she corrects him, he will never change. She cannot see that Andy's limitations are what make him human and lovable in the first place. While there are things that Andy needs to change for his own sake, Liz's constant criticism often encourages him to resist that change. It makes him feel threatened and insecure.

When limitations are accepted, a relationship feels comfortable and safe. Sharon and Ken have such a marriage. There is a give-and-take, a respect, an acceptance. Sharon has always been scatterbrained, especially where money is concerned. Ken simply laughs, accepts this limitation, and puts her on an allowance to avoid financial chaos. When Sharon turned fifty and decided to try new things, Ken encouraged her. She took up skating and broke her foot. She took up art lessons and finished nary a painting,

Both Ken and Sharon laughed at her inability to learn and follow through on these ventures. And Ken continued to support her as she moved on to the next thing.

For Ken and Sharon, the support is mutual. Their interests, except for the children, are polar opposites.

Ken is a thinker, Sharon a doer. At fifty, Sharon tucked two master's degrees under her arm and headed back to school for a doctorate. Ken bought a boat and a pickup and began an earnest pursuit of his favorite pastime, fishing. A clear-cut conflict of interest, to be sure. Ken had never finished high school, yet he was an avid reader. So when Sharon was struggling through her journey to Canterbury, Ken often came to her rescue. He waded through the mire of Old English right behind her, deciphering and learning with her as they went along. Meanwhile Sharon, perennial creature of comfort, waded bravely through the mire of the backwoods, squeamishly learning to bait her own hook. It has taken some adjustment, a lot of give-and-take. It has taken a lot of work, a lot of investing.

It is this investment, by both partners, that gives a relationship value—a sense of something ongoing, not momentary. Neither Sharon nor Ken sees that one is right and the other wrong. Instead each tries to adjust to the other's way of life. They accept, cooperate, and compromise, trusting that they will continue to care and be cared for.

This trust gets a couple over the bumps—the frustrations, disappointments, and conflicts—in one piece, together. When Connie and David bought their first home, they slaved side by side to make it livable. On hands and knees, they sanded and stained the hardwood floors, then poured a glass of wine to celebrate just before the spring shower hit. Aghast, they watched as water seeped through their freshly painted ceiling, threatening to destroy their handiwork before the floors even dried. David stormed out the back door for a large tarp in the garage to minimize the damage. In his desperate attempt to manage the back door, the fifty-pound tarp, and the rain, he cut his arm on the screen. "Connie, Connie!" he called calmly from the back door. Running to the kitchen, Connie saw him drenched and bleeding, with the tarp heaped at his feet. "I'm leaving now," he said in mock seriousness. "You can keep the house!" "All I could think of," Connie laughs as she relates the story, "was 'how *dare* he even *think* of leaving me with this monstrosity,' knowing full well he wasn't going anywhere."

This kind of trust in a relationship is built one step at a time, inch by painstaking inch. It develops primarily through experience with the other person. It comes from moving through the periods of closeness, separateness, and isolation enough times to trust—even in the most distant periods—that your partner cares and will be back. We cannot always care for our partner, not because we are untrustworthy but because of where we are as individuals at any given time. But as we build a relationship, we develop a sense of trust that most of the time, say at least three weeks out of every four, we can depend on our partner's ability to care for us and vice versa.

This trust is essential to withstand the strain of inevitable crisis. Because she did not believe, did not trust, that she could share life's problems with her husband, Darrell, Sara was forced to assume total responsibility for herself and the family. Darrell, she had found through experience after experience, could not be counted on. When it came to keeping a job, being home when the children were sick, or just sharing life's ups and downs, he couldn't, wasn't, and didn't. Instead he could usually be found out drinking with the boys or, in a pinch, alone. Already in serious trouble, their marriage was shaken even further when Sara found she required surgery.

"Please," she pleaded with Darrell. "Just this once, don't drink while I'm away. I need to depend on you to take care of the children and me during this time. I really need to trust that you will stand by and help me through this." He assured her that he would take care of everything. But when Sara came out of the anesthetic in her hospital room, she found herself alone. Where was Darrell? Three hours later, after a quick beer with the guys at the office, he appeared. The last ounce of trust had been violated. With that gone, there was no answer for Sara but divorce. For without trust, love dies.

How do we build this trust in a relationship? We begin by doing, by first trusting our partner and experiencing his or her response. Carla and Mike had been married for almost three years. While they truly shared their lives—work, household chores, money—Carla did not feel that she could trust Mike to be there if she needed him. And she was afraid to test that feeling because she was afraid she might be right! In truth, Mike was trustworthy and had shown that he was repeatedly. It was Carla's fear that he would let her down that held her back. As I encouraged her to trust her feelings with Mike, to really tell him how she felt, Carla began to see that her fears were unfounded. Once, when she had been deeply hurt by a friend and felt she had no one to share her grief, she turned to Mike. She dreaded sharing her feelings with him, fearing that he wouldn't listen, wouldn't care, wouldn't understand. But he did listen and care that she was hurt. And when she cried, he was there to hold and comfort her.

Notice that I did not say that he was there to take care of her. When I speak of caring for someone in a trusting way, I do not mean taking care of the person. Many people equate caring with giving people answers to their problems. To care in the way I am talking about is to trust that the other person can work out his or her own problems, while caring enough to listen and support that person.

Laurie had quit trying to share her feelings with Keith because she felt that he treated her like a child. She could not trust that he would be helpful, supportive, caring. Concerned about their son, she would say, "I'm so upset about Sammy. He doesn't seem to make friends." Keith would respond, "You must make him go out and play with other children. If you didn't let him watch TV so much, he would make friends. You get so upset over every little thing. Quit worrying so much. He'll be all right." End of conversation.

Laurie felt belittled. Keith did not understand, or respect, or care about her feelings. As I worked with Keith and Laurie, and they began to learn how to share and trust each other, the scenario came out quite differently. When Laurie expresses concern about their son, Keith now listens and asks more questions about the way Laurie feels and why she feels that way. Then the two of them, together, decide how to handle the problem. Keith now sees that Laurie was asking for understanding and support, not answers. And he has found, along with Laurie, that when they trust each other enough to share their feelings, they usually come up with a better answer—whatever the problem. No one wants a caretaker. But we all want to trust that we can be seen and respected as a person and that our partner will care for and stand by that person.

Love also involves that feeling of intensity we talked about earlier, that hunger for the other person. This intensity comes from our very core, where our feelings run the deepest. Where, "It feels so good to touch

you." Where, "It hurts when you are mad at me."
Where, "I feel so happy just sitting here with you."
Where, "I want to work it out so much I can't sleep."
We really hunger for the other person when we love
him or her. It hurts in our very depth when we feel
isolated from our partner—a deep hurt, not simply
loneliness.

Acceptance, trust, intensity—all are part of loving.
Yet it is difficult to pinpoint the ingredient that makes
love different, more than any of these. So far, I have
been straight and sincere about knowing and not
knowing. At this point, I want to cheat and say intensity is it. This is the quality that distinguishes real
love. This is what sets it apart from all the other feelings. But I can't. Wait. Maybe I can. I was thinking
that I have felt this intensity with very close friends
whom I certainly had no desire to marry. But that
doesn't mean it isn't love. It just means that it has
not developed to that degree. Maybe that is it. Maybe
it is a matter of degree.

Kathy's relationship with three different men, only
one of whom she loves, clearly illustrates the puzzle.
Dave is someone she has been close to since college.
He is a person she shares with and cares about. And
the degree of caring is very great. He and she both
accept the other and feel a real degree of intensity
when they are together. But she does not miss him—
she does not hurt—when they are apart. Jerry is fun,
a person she shares with and cares for. But the degree
of intensity is not there.

Rick is someone she shares with, cares for, and is
intensely involved with. She waits for his call, hurts
when he hurts, feels a sense of joy when she is with
him. There's no doubt about it. She loves him. But
why Rick? Why not Dave or Jerry? What is the ingredient that makes the difference? It is not the sharing or caring or even the commitment. It is the degree

of intensity in the relationship. So if we boil it all down, that is it. It is the degree. But why did it develop with Rick and not with Jerry or Dave? Both Kathy and Rick wanted it from each other at the same time. They are both capable. So are Jerry and Dave. But it is with Rick that it developed.

Back to biology, to chemistry, to psychology. Back to the mystery, ultimately, that brings two people through all of these stages to the point of love.

And perhaps, just perhaps, back to a little bit of magic!

3

The Big Three

It is with some well-justified ambivalence, if not outright trepidation, that we look upon this thing called "love." It's the fickle stuff of broken hearts and dreams, after all. It appears to be the bedrock of our Gross National Product as well, keeping a host of industries going—from recording studios and rock stars to deodorants and discos. We sidestep the issue, trying to convince ourselves that "love" is a luxury item—something we can take or leave, something we simply *want*—when, in fact, it is something we need. Our apprehension is understandable because, most assuredly, there is a price to be paid, a cost-benefit ratio to be considered!

We all know the push-pull of these emotions, the attraction and repulsion of the forces that seem to compel us to establish contact, to form relationships with others. It is fundamental. It is human. It is the perennial tug-of-war between our need for warmth, for closeness, for intimacy and our need for safety, for control, for security. The ability to balance these apparently diametrically opposed needs permits a relationship to develop. It permits any relationship—acquaintances, co-workers, friends! In any interaction between two people, there is this balance, this trade-off, between intimacy and security, between risking openness and preserving safety, between gambling on closeness and jeopardizing control.

This dynamic tension exists in all relationships. And that makes it difficult enough to maintain "balance" with all of those people who are valuable to us, who inhabit our world: our friends, our family, our bosses, our colleagues, our clients, our postman. But in the most primary of our relationships, in our marriage, this balance is even more delicate, more precarious, more critical. Because into the mix we throw the third basic need: sex.

Sex? Yes, sex, *not* to be confused with intimacy. Sex may have everything or nothing to do with intimacy, with friendship, with love. As frightening, as risky, as intimacy is, we are relatively generous with it. Because the balance is between only two needs, intimacy and security, we can be more open, risk more, in nonsexual relationships. We care for, even love, many. We can afford to because there is a threshold, a line drawn around the core of us, that only a very few may cross. And sex is one important mode of transportation. It is both a symbolic and literal "opening up" to another human being. It is, by its very nature, an act of trust. We are vulnerable. We are exposed.

Sex has many roles, many purposes, in our society and in our personal lives. It provides different things for different people at different times—many good things, some bad things. It is not my purpose here to discuss sex in any of these contexts. Others before me have covered that territory quite well. Nor is it my purpose to discuss, really, sex in the physical sense.

Again, there are many excellent books on that subject. My purpose is to put sex in perspective, to help couples understand its place and its critical importance in a committed, loving relationship; its relationship to intimacy and security; the whys and wherefores of its ebb and flow. For perhaps, more than either of the other basic needs, sex is situational. It can be discussed *only* in some context. It can be lewd. It can be almost holy. And so, I will be discussing sex in the context of "lovers" in the fullest sense of the word, committed partners. This is sex for the very married. In this context, in the marriage relationship, sex relates decidedly to the balance of intimacy and security. The elements are inextricably linked.

But how? At first glance, the relationship of these three basic elements may seem quite simple. They balance seesaw fashion at two opposing poles, with intimacy and sexual involvement at one pole and security at the other. After all, such apparently conflicting needs surely require a trade-off of one type or another to establish balance. Isn't to be totally intimate and sexual to be totally insecure? Isn't to be totally secure to be nonintimate and asexual? No, on both counts. Certainly, the more we risk being close—being intimate, being sexual—with another human being, the more we stand to lose. And yet, paradoxically, the greater the degree of intimacy—of trust, of commitment—we have established with another, the more secure we become.

This hardly seems possible! But if we look at the relationship between these three elements more closely, we begin to see them not as opposing forces but as a unified whole. It may be helpful to visualize all three bound together in a circular pattern—constantly flowing like a juggling act. As in any dynamic process, a shift in any *one* of these elements creates a change in the other. A *change*, yes. But not necessarily an *exchange*, or trade-off. To have more of one thing, we don't necessarily have to give up something else. The truth is that in marriage, perhaps more readily than in any other relationship, we can have it all. Quite unexpectedly, we find that security can enhance intimacy—and sex! And vice versa! A little juggling is required, to be sure. But if you don't know how, you can learn. As any experienced juggler can tell you, the secret is all in the wrist.

SECURITY: GETTING YOURS AND KEEPING IT

Rumor has it that security is enjoying a return to vogue. On college campuses, the barometers of social change, philosophy majors are about as scarce as shoulder-length hair on men. "Marketable" degrees—in engineering, communications, business—are eagerly pursued as the best insurance in the "real world," and the future job, versus the education, is rapidly becoming the major emphasis.

But I'm talking about security in a larger sense—not just material security but personal security, not net worth but self-worth. And its importance and value have never really waned. In fact, *insecure* is a very nasty word in our society. We often hear people remark in a derogatory manner, "I feel so terribly insecure today," or, "He's one of the most insecure people I've ever met," as though insecurity is the most disagreeable of human conditions, as if total security is the ultimate goal. I have to smile because absolute security is death, either physical or emotional.

In the midst of a therapy group I once conducted, a young woman announced with great pride, "I have finally reached the point where I never feel insecure. I feel totally calm and at peace. Nothing is ever going to threaten my sense of security again." Nirvana at last! She smiled a Mona Lisa smile and sat back, expecting everyone to congratulate her on her new-found state of grace. What a surprise she got when the general response was, "What happened? Did you have a lobotomy over the weekend?" Quite miffed, the woman asked, "Do you mean that total security is not the objective here? I thought that was the goal!"

Like many people in our society, this woman equated security with maturity and sound mental health. Certainly, we must experience some degree of security to function. But, in contrast, we must accept a degree of insecurity to really live. This is particularly true in intimate relationships. As we explained to this woman, the goal is to feel secure enough about ourselves that we can reach out for more involvement, more intimacy, with others. But that does not eliminate our sense of insecurity. Each and every time we open up to others—to our spouse, to anyone—we are risking something. Each time we reveal something, expose ourselves emotionally or sexually, our sense of security is threatened. When we reach out sexually, we fear rejection. When we reach out emotionally, we fear misunderstanding.

But reach we do because these needs for intimacy, and sex, are basic. They are human. And they cannot be satisfied from within. Facts are facts. We are not self-contained. But to place the satisfaction of these very important needs in the hands of another is very anxiety producing, very threatening. We are relinquishing total control. It is out of our hands, temporarily. That's part of the juggling act: entrusting another with our needs for sex and intimacy while retaining a sense of security in the process. Only by denying these needs can we feel totally secure. Getting involved, either emotionally or sexually, *is* risky. We risk our feeling of security.

There are ways around this. But it usually requires some pretty elaborate mental acrobatics to hide the truth from ourselves! When we were younger, say in high school, we used to "go steady," frankly, for one reason: to feel more secure. But we told ourselves that it was love. We were committed only. But that commitment gave us the security to experiment with both intimacy and sex. A bit later, at the dawn of the sexual revolution, we used this sort of relationship (though by now we called it something else, like being dropped, or pinned or even engaged) to explore a more complete sexual relationship with another person.

Having grown up with a myriad of superstitions, dictates, and taboos surrounding sex, women in particular often use these outward trappings of commitment as shields against the guilt they have been so thoroughly taught to associate with sex. And who's to say that's bad? As one young woman, who had a series of relatively committed, relatively long-term, and absolutely exclusive sexual relationships, explained, "That kind of arrangement kept me from feeling like a prostitute." Because these relationships, by virtue of their relative longevity and exclusivity, were socially sanctioned somewhat, this woman was able to explore her own sexuality and develop a very uninhibited, natural, and healthy attitude toward sex. This woman's experience provides an important clue to the secret of this juggling act. Contrary to our initial supposition that security is directly opposed to intimacy and sex, we find that it may actually *contribute* to the satisfaction of these two needs.

From this perspective it would seem that the most ideal context in which sex and intimacy might flourish is marriage, for marriage, and the commitment it carries, increases our security. And this sanctioned relationship *does* give some couples the security they need to be more open, more intimate, more sexual with one another. But what about the rest? Why do so many couples fail to use this most nurturing and supportive of relationships to cultivate intimacy and sexual openness?

The truth is that often we are so busy trying to preserve our security in the marriage that we actually curb all risk-taking activity. We stick to what has worked in the past sexually. We tend to take what we can get and be thankful for it. We are so happy to finally feel secure that we say, in effect, "Whew! Thank God! Now I can relax."

We are lulled by our sense of security into believing that this is our only, or most important, need. That's what Diane and Jeff believed, until their separation, that is.

Only then were they able to regain their perspective, to acknowledge their needs for intimacy and sex, to admit those needs to one another, and to work toward satisfying them. It took the separation, the ultimate threat to security, to jog them out of their rut. It took that threat to awaken them to the realization that you can't feel intimate and sexual (that is, alive) without feeling insecure, without taking risks to improve the relationship. It took that realization to make Diane and Jeff look at what they wanted and needed in a fresh, new way. For example, one thing they wanted was a better sexual relationship. Both were dissatisfied. But neither could admit it. That would be a terrible breach of security! Diane rarely shared Jeff's sexual interest because she got nothing for herself from the experience. She missed the kissing and the petting they enjoyed before they were married. She missed the teasing and the laughing and the playing. But she never told Jeff. As is typical of many couples, all that "kid stuff" ended the day they were married. There was nothing left but sexual intercourse. And that seemed to be enough for Jeff. So Diane went along with his demands, meeting his needs while never articulating hers. She was afraid to tell Jeff how unhappy she was—afraid he would be hurt, afraid he would turn away from her, afraid he would take away some of her security.

And Jeff was afraid to tell Diane that making love with her was like going to bed with a robot, for all the same reasons. But their separation wiped out all excuses about security. So they began cultivating the other things they needed: intimacy, sex. When both Diane and Jeff admitted that sex was no fun for anybody, they could begin to learn to make love in a new way by being more open about their feelings. They started off each day with kissing and caressing each other, then added, not substituted, sexual intercourse. Both learned new ways to enjoy sex each and every time because sex was different each time. And so were their feelings.

Diane and Jeff are no longer afraid of these shifts in the balance of their needs. They are secure, in the only real sense of the word. They have the security that comes from a *trust* in one another's continued caring and commitment to an open, honest, intimate relationship. Theirs is *not* the false security, the "locked in" security that they once thought would keep their marriage safe. It took the separation, with its threat of divorce, to make Diane and Jeff realize that marriage doesn't come with any lifetime guarantee. Yet many people go into marriage expecting just that, believing in a security that does not exist.

That kind of security comes only with invulnerability and control. And imposing those sorts of reins on a marriage can make it a docile creature indeed. They choke life and vitality, for they deny our needs. The more rein we give ourselves and our relationship —the more we allow ourselves to need intimacy, sex, and each other—the less control we have. The more we risk in allowing ourselves to need another person, the more insecure we become. After all, we just might not get those needs met! But it's a cinch they won't be met if we never give the other person a chance. Many years ago I thought that the way out of this predicament was to only *want* to be close, not to really *need* being close. Impossible. All that holding back makes possible is playing it safe. It interferes with the degree of intimacy we can share with another person. It puts up barriers to closeness.

INTIMACY: UPPING THE ANTE

Sometimes these barriers are quite invisible, even to our own eyes. But they protect us from risk and shield us from true intimacy. We send out all sorts of clever decoys. We wrap ourselves protectively in our little white lies until we begin to believe that they are the truth. We deny that we have real feelings, real needs, underneath those roles we don each morning. And we settle for something less than we need, then pretend we didn't need more in the first place.

But we do need more. We need the intensity, the openness, the trust, the honesty of an intimate relationship. We need a person with whom we can be this free—a person with whom we can shed all the roles we must play in a given day; a person with whom we can be vulnerable, soft, tender, needy, angry, childish. In short, we need a person with whom we can be totally ourselves.

When I speak of the need for intimacy, I am not talking about total dependency, the kind associated with what we in the South call a clinging vine, the type of woman who literally cannot function unless she's entwined around a man's arm. This is not intimacy but infancy. Just as a vine can choke the life out of a tree, so the kind of woman (or man!) who clings to a partner can choke the life out of a relationship.

It is suicide for a loving relationship. But it does make for a secure one. The clinging vine believes that her husband will not leave her because she could not function without him. And her husband knows that she is totally dependent on his care and protection.

I can assure you that this syndrome is not limited to the southern belle. Kim, in fact, was from New England. She and Harry married quite young. And the marriage was the great escape for both of them. Kim had been totally cared for by overindulgent but demanding parents. Harry, in contrast, had to do everything for himself and his aging mother. Both were looking for a way out. And marriage looked like the ticket. They were in love. Their problems were over.

But, not-so-oddly enough, very little changed after the wedding. Harry became the dominating "parent" who took care of the childlike Kim, even after they had two children of their own. He managed all the errand running—shopping for groceries, shuttling the children to school, and so on—in addition to his demanding fifty-hour-a-week job. He was seldom home. Kim, on the other hand, almost never left the house, content to cook, clean, and tend the children twenty-four hours a day, seven days a week. Her life was restricted almost to the point of nonfunctioning.

One morning, when they were thirty-five years old, Harry decided that Kim was a burden he didn't need and left her with the admonition, "Grow up." And rather than wither away, Kim began to do just that. Once out from under Harry's overprotective thumb, Kim began to blossom. Not basically a clinging vine, Kim was an underdeveloped child who needed only encouragement and support to grow. Today, two years later, Kim is very much an adult. She has assumed responsibility for herself and two young children. She has a full-time job and an active social life. She is involved with a man whom she loves, though she plans to wait at least two years before remarrying. She is willing to risk and now sees life as a great adventure. Of course, she is often insecure. But she is also intimate with friends and lovers and is able to experience sex as an adult. She is one of the most complete human beings I have worked with. She can balance the three needs—security, intimacy, and sex—with courage and excitement, but not without fear. Her openness to experiencing life has helped her, at last, to grow up.

Harry, on the other hand, has managed to find another clinging vine to marry and is repeating the same pattern with a second wife. As it turned out (as it often does), it was Harry—apparently strong, apparently healthy Harry—who needed the security of taking care of, and controlling, a relationship to function. Control is the lifeblood of security and the death of intimacy. Relinquishing that control, exposing ourselves emotionally and physically to another, takes courage, for true courage means risking in spite of our fear that we will be rejected or found wanting.

From the outside looking in, Sandy and Skip exemplified this type of courage. They appeared to be risking everything, going for broke in their marriage. It was the second for each of them, so both were determined to succeed this time around. Sandy, in particular, seemed very courageous in her demands for closeness and intimacy. Even I thought so. She kept pushing on Skip, demanding more from him and from their relationship. And I kept encouraging her and offering support.

So I was taken by surprise, one day, when Sandy called asking to see me. "I'm feeling afraid," she said. "I want more from Skip. But I'm scared to push it." Sandy's fear was a new one on me! But as I tried to discover its basis, I finally understood: Sandy had always skirted the issue. She had not been courageous. She had played it safe. She had never really permitted herself to *need* Skip, telling herself instead that divorce was always an option if the marriage didn't work out. She did not allow herself to become interdependent with Skip, to jeopardize her own safety.

But now she was finally permitting herself to need Skip, to want more from him and give more herself. The stakes were getting higher. And now she had to muster true courage, to acknowledge her need for Skip and take the necessary risks in spite of her fears.

For instance, when Skip's work took him out of town for several days at a time, they had to maintain their relationship by telephone. And Sandy found their telephone conversations most unsatisfactory. Skip would call home to tell Sandy how upset or excited, or whatever, he was. And she would listen and be supportive. But when she would try to tell him how she was feeling or how her day was going, Skip would interrupt with, "Sorry, I've got to get to that meeting [or to dinner with this or that client]. We'll talk about this later, okay?" Well, it was *not* okay with Sandy. She felt that they were meeting Skip's needs but not hers. And she told him so. They discussed it at length and agreed that on the next trip Skip would call only when there was time to discuss Sandy's needs as well as his. They went over it three times, and Sandy felt certain that when Skip called from a distant town the next morning, their conversation would be different. It wasn't. Skip called, all right, to tell Sandy all about how unsure he felt about his upcoming presentation at the morning's meeting. As usual, Sandy listened and offered her support and encouragement. But just when she began to tell Skip about her morning, he said, "Oh, I wish I could listen. But the meeting is starting in a few minutes, and I have to run!"

Sandy was mad but thought, "Now hold on. Naturally, he is anxious about this morning. Let's wait until he calls again before we jump to conclusions." Her chance to jump came that night, when Skip called *just* to tell her that everything had gone well at the meeting, that she had really helped him that morning, and that he had to rush to a client dinner but would be home the next night.

It was as though they had never had their discussions about two-way telephone conversations. That did it. Sandy told him just what she thought: He was self-centered; he was not interested in her needs; he only used her as a support system. Then she slammed the receiver in his ear.

Skip called right back, and, one hour and $12.70 worth of change later, they began to straighten things out. But the incident was enough to give Sandy a good scare. It showed her how much she really needed Skip, how much his lack of sensitivity could hurt her, and how insecure her need for intimacy, for closeness, made her.

The deeper we move into a relationship, as Sandy was doing in her marriage, the more is at stake. The more interdependent we are, the more we permit ourselves to need from another person, the higher the price in security. The more we love, the more painful it is to have that love go unreturned. Becoming secure enough within ourselves to relinquish control, to risk being open and intimate in our relationships, is difficult under any circumstances. And marriage is, paradoxically, the most difficult and the most ideal of circumstances for doing just that. It is the most difficult because, after all, we're getting a lot out of this deal! The high stakes encourage us to play it safe, maintain control, avoid risks. And it is the most ideal because of the very security and trust that these same high stakes—commitment, intimacy, love—foster.

This duality of the marriage relationship enables us

to feel, simultaneously, our most secure and our most vulnerable. And nowhere is the conflict of these two feelings, the need for intimacy and the desire for security, more apparent than in our sexual relationship with our spouse.

SEX: INTO THE FIRE

Someone once said, "When a marriage goes on the rocks, the first place to check is the mattress." To let you know where I stand from the outset, my only comment on that is "*Ridiculous!*" Sex, or more appropriately, sexual attraction and response to a spouse, is the barometer of a relationship. It reflects the ups and downs, the highs and lows, of a couple's relationship. It does not cause them. Sexual desire and response are outgrowths both of feelings of closeness *and* safety, intimacy *and* security.

Sex is not intimacy. It may contribute to it, but it cannot substitute for it. Sexual expression is the natural extension of our desire to be close to the person we love. Yet to risk the openness of total (not just *physical!*) sexual expression, we must feel secure enough in our relationship to "turn ourselves loose," so to speak, to welcome the intensity of such an encounter. When either of these elements flounders, when the balance is upset, mysterious lumps spring up in the mattress overnight.

But sex doesn't start or end on that mattress. Sex is not a discrete act at a discrete time in a discrete place. It is a continual interchange in a marriage. It is what changes us from friends into lovers. It is not the be-all and end-all of a relationship. It is only one of the basic ingredients. So I'm not going to say much about sex "below the waist" but, rather, will approach sex from the head down, which is the way it flows in a loving relationship. In fact, I'm not even going to mention sexual techniques, for each couple's techniques are unique. While there are just so many physical ways to make love, the expression of physical love in response to individual desires, expectations, and needs is different for each person, each time, in each situation. It is not for me or anyone else to dictate. It is for each and every couple that ever was or will be to explore. So I encourage each couple to discover their own techniques for expressing their love for each other in a physical way, their own ways of adventuring together, their own approach to finding new ways of being sexual with one another. And that requires, more than a liberated body, an open mind—one swept clean of all the myths, the rules, the illusions we have inherited with respect to sex.

"Now what *is* this woman talking about?" you're probably wondering. Yes, I know we had a sexual revolution. And, yes, I know that all these myths are supposedly behind us. And, yes, many of the physiological myths *have* been dispelled. Thanks to the excellent work of several modern sex researchers, we are freer in the physical sense. We are free from ignorance. We are on friendlier terms with our bodies. We are less afraid of them.

But in another way this sexual revolution, like its industrial counterpart, has only further entrenched the attitude of body as machine. Push button A, get response B. This attitude encourages us to see our partners as sexual robots, as stereotypes, not as the unique individuals we married in the first place. We disassociate our "selves"—our mind, our emotions—from our bodies. But to fully experience the joy of a sexual encounter, these two must be integrated. So I'm going to dispense with the physical myths that others have buried so well and focus on some of the psychological myths that still keep us from what I think of as the human, versus mechanical, experience of sex—

myths that hamper growth and expression in this most intense of human encounters. Here are just a few.

1. *Men have all the marbles.* In spite of the fatal wounding of the "experienced groom and virgin bride" myth during the sexual revolution, this particular myth remains virtually unscathed. A "real" man should know all about sex before marriage and serve as chief mentor for the woman. Notice that teacher and student roles are built right in, which gives everyone concerned something nice and secure to fall back on. These roles give us a sense that *someone,* at least, knows what to do. And that's a lot more secure than both realizing, and admitting, that we are ignorant—perhaps not of technique but most certainly of each other. Each woman's (and, surprise, surprise, man's) sexual needs are different. Each requires special, unique attention and understanding. Sexual expression requires learning and, yes, practice. But, ideally, in the marriage relationship the trust and intimacy we have built gives us the security we need to be open with one another in this way. If both partners see learning about sex, about each other's individual needs, as an adventure, security is not threatened.

2. *Sex is serious business.* Sometimes. Sometimes it is playful. And sometimes it is downright silly. It may be making love behind a secluded sand dune after a moonlit swim and game of tag on the beach. Or it may be a game of gin rummy, in which every point entitles the winner to one whole minute of his or her favorite sexual activity. Or it may be a secret luncheon rendezvous for a make-believe affair with your hus-

band or wife. Or it may be a surprise greeting in seductive attire. With imagination as the only prop, sexual encounter is the ideal stage on which to indulge even our most absurd or childish fantasies. This is the time and the place to pretend, to "play like," and to explore, through playing, all facets of ourselves and each other.

3. *Sex belongs under the covers, in the dark.* Sex is a twenty-four-hour-a-day thing. It is continuous. It can't be separated out and tucked under the covers for thirty minutes twice a week. Sex is the loving expression of our attraction to another person. Sex is our physical sharing with that person on many levels, from just walking together and holding hands to snuggling under the covers. It is an expression of our caring, of our commitment, of our love. Without this sharing in the daytime, nighttime sharing becomes increasingly sporadic and perfunctory. We must be aware of the need to express our love, to touch and kiss, long before we ever reach the bedroom. Both men and women need this physical closeness, this reassurance that they are cared for and loved by the other. Too often, the "little" expressions of love—the touching, the kissing, the holding hands—end the day of the wedding. But it is these very expressions of tenderness, *daily*, that are essential to remind ourselves that it is this unique person whom we love and desire.

4. *Not* everything *is normal, you know!* Maybe not. But almost anything that gives pleasure without harm to both partners *is* quite normal, and healthy. Finding out just what these things are, for both partners, is half the fun. The bedroom is one of the most important places to throw out all the "shoulds" and "shouldn'ts," the "nice"

and "not nice" rules we inherited, and make up our own rules. Again, marriage is the ideal relationship in which to do just this because mutual trust and acceptance give us the security to *ask* for what we want and need and to give what our partner asks in return. This kind of emotional nakedness makes us far more vulnerable than physical exposure. It also, if we can muster the courage to risk this type of honesty and openness, brings us far closer to each other than mere physical contact ever could.

5. *Bodies get boring.* In other words, we can get too familiar with each other as sexual partners. Impossible. Quite the opposite, in fact, seems to hold true. As we get used to each other, we come to know one another's needs better. We learn the little secrets of pleasing each other. We learn just what tricks make that other body we are so fond of *particularly* happy! We trust more. We become less inhibited. The frenzy dies. The pleasure begins. In fact, sex actually begins to improve during our mid thirties, if we are receptive to change. Male and female sex drives, at odds in terms of level until this point, tend to synchronize. And we begin to feel more adventurous in our sexual experiences.

Certainly, the frequency of sexual intercourse declines as we grow older. But the intensity of the encounter increases as we learn to express our love in the physical manner that means the very most to our partner, engendering the response that means the most to us. Here again, we must learn how to express our love in a way the other person can appreciate and understand. That means asking what is pleasurable when we don't know and speaking up when we do or don't particularly enjoy something. It is this learning—this constant changing, exploring, and growing in our sexual expression—that keeps this aspect of a relationship alive and vital.

6. *Men are ready for sex at any time.* (Corollary myth: Women need to be in the mood!) This particular myth, a direct offshoot of the "man as machine" theory, does a great disservice to men. A man's need, and desire, for sex is as much related to his feelings, to the situation, and to his emotions as a woman's need and desire. For example, if a man is upset about something at the office, he is probably not going to be interested in a sexual experience. Sex, for men as well as for women, is rooted above, not below, the belt. That's what makes it human.

7. *No one wants to be a sex object!* Says who? Marilyn, a very successful and intelligent young career woman more than capable of taking care of herself, thank you, very facetiously summed it up during a discussion with one of her also quite self-sufficient friends: "After all our demands that men appreciate us for our brains and our accomplishments, all we *really* want is to be loved for our bodies!" *Of course*, women want to be seen and understood and appreciated as individuals. But they also very much want, and need, to have their sexuality affirmed. They *are* sexual beings. And they are enjoying their own and their partner's growing appreciation of that fact.

Men, too (down with another myth!), need to have their sexuality affirmed as much as the fairer sex! Their masculinity, their pride in themselves as men, depends on the female response to their maleness. Again, sex per se is not the only facet of their being that men want to have appreciated. But it is an important one.

Women are only now beginning to see or, at any rate, openly acknowledge their men as sexual beings, affirming their maleness both verbally and nonverbally. And this healthy delight by both men and women in one another's bodies is both contributing to and demanding more from today's marriages.

8. *An ego is a very fragile thing, especially where sex is concerned!* This persistent myth binds both the man and the woman to ignorance and, ultimately, to boredom. A woman who expects her partner to understand her sexual needs intuitively, who is afraid to express her desires, never gets what she wants. Most men and women want to please their partners sexually, to express their love in a way that the other will understand. But women—and men!—must first speak up! Surprisingly, egos are pretty sturdy things. And open, frank discussions of sexual needs enhance both security and trust and, hence, freedom to move toward increased intimacy.

9. *Lack of orgasms can be hazardous to your health.* After many years of beating down the myth that women are not supposed to enjoy sex, a brand-new myth has arisen to take its place: the myth of the "Big O." O for "orgasm." O for "orbit." Because of women's slightly more subtle physiology, this persistent myth is particularly hard on them. Today, many couples feel that if a woman does not experience multiple orgasms, or at *least* one, with each encounter, the couple has failed miserably. The truth is that many times a woman (and sometimes a man) enjoys the pleasing sexual experience for just the sense of physical closeness. At other times, she may require one or several orgasms

to release sexual tension. Sex is never the same and changes each and every time. And each experience can be a satisfying one if we don't try to force ourselves into expected responses, if we remember that the best orgasms are the ones right here on earth, in our lover's arms, as intensely aware of him or her as we are of ourselves.

10. *After age fifty-five the thrill is gone.* People over fifty-five find this myth particularly amusing. Certainly, there are some physical changes as we grow older. For instance, a man may or may not experience an orgasm with each sexual encounter. But these changes need not hamper our enjoyment, for the experience of sex is no different. As with any delicate, elegant apparatus, our sexual equipment requires continued use to remain in good working condition. And the more sexually active we continue to be, the less physical change there is. So continued sex is important for sex to continue. And continue it can, into our eighties and nineties.

Sweeping out these and other psychological myths that we still harbor about sex goes a long way toward eliminating all those physiological ones as well. It frees us to explore, understand, and use our own bodies to the fullest. And the more we know, the freer we are. Ignorance is confining. It holds us to established patterns. It stifles expression. Our sexual relationship is reduced to a series of well-entrenched responses. Some people call them ruts.

George and Cindy had been in one for the entire seven years of their marriage. They married, after three years of steady dating, when they were only eighteen. They were very young and totally inexperienced sexually. They were both shy and insecure and inhibited. And, after seven years, little had changed. Cindy was so trapped by her need for security that she could not allow herself to be sexual. So inhibited was she that George had never seen her nude. She had never even looked at a human body, his or her own! George, too, was afraid to venture out. He was so angry and felt so rejected that he had completely withdrawn. But ultimately it was George's need for intimacy and sexual response that overcame his need for security. He had to begin. But where? George didn't know. Cindy *certainly* didn't know. And that very lack of knowledge was the solution to the problem: George and Cindy both admitted that they knew nothing about sex and wanted to learn. That freed them by giving them a basis for security, their shared innocence. From that, they could begin learning about sex together. As they began sharing their feelings, their fears, their desires—even their shyness!—their sexual relationship began to fall into place.

George quit shielding Cindy from his sexual needs, and Cindy began to shed her inhibitions and respond to George as an adult. In working with George and Cindy, as I do with most couples who come to see me for sexual counseling, I do not focus on sexual technique. Instead I encourage these couples to make an adventure out of learning and discovering—even inventing!—those techniques most pleasurable to them. I have found many excellent books on the market that provide this freedom for those individuals in need of sex education only. But none of these books can really solve a true sexual problem. Just as are sexual pleasures, sexual problems are generally rooted above the belt and require professional help to resolve.

Increasingly, couples are accepting and seeking that help. Sexual problems, for men and women, are nothing new. They are, however, coming to light more frequently because only now are we beginning to speak of sex openly. Only now are we beginning to realize that we don't have to be satisfied with an unsatisfactory sexual response. Only now are we realizing that most of these problems can be corrected. Only now are we becoming receptive to help. Rather than a sign of trouble, seeking help is often a very healthy sign that a couple is working on their marriage.

Chris and Patrick came to me after ten years of marriage for one reason: to improve their sexual relationship. Chris had never reached orgasm, and Patrick reached it too quickly. Both were attractive, intelligent, well-educated people—she, a biochemist, and he, a successful businessman. Together they had read many books on sexual technique, trying to use them as self-help manuals without success. They needed a different approach.

For Chris, sex education and encouragement were sufficient to clear up the problem. I suggested, after a session of plain "birds and the bees" sex education, that she go home and spend time getting to know, and feeling comfortable with, her own body. She had never even looked at it in the mirror, except in passing. She took my instructions seriously and, with Patrick's support, began to get acquainted with her own body and her sexuality.

To solve Patrick's problem, we simply taught him and Chris a very simple technique for controlling the timing of his sexual release, or orgasm, thus putting him back in charge of his sexual experience. Using this technique, Patrick discovered that he had been missing more than half the fun and excitement of sex by concentrating almost exclusively on intercourse and, specifically, his orgasm. He had never known the joys of just touching and discovering and enjoying Chris. He was the one who came in one day saying, "I never knew Chris was so beautiful or sexual. What a joy this is!"

Chris and Patrick had special problems, which required special, individualized, professional attention. They learned the specific techniques that worked for them. They learned about orgasm and sexual response. But, more important, they learned about touching and holding, the cornerstones of intimacy. They discovered the sheer pleasure of physical closeness, not just sex.

It is this closeness, this heightened intimacy, that makes sex such a valuable part of the marriage relationship. It is the complete trust in our partner at our most vulnerable moments, in sexual embrace, that is the hallmark of our love and commitment to one another. And that is why, in the face of shifting mores and sexual values, I strongly feel that the concept that we have come to know as "open marriage"—that is, a commitment that does not involve sexual exclusivity —can only undermine the type of relationship I am describing.

Pulling one of these basic elements, sex or intimacy or security, from a relationship disturbs the balance of the relationship. The absence or distortion or diminishing of one affects the others. The elements reinforce one another. Our desire for intimacy draws us into the marriage alliance in the first place. Ideally, the trust, the acceptance, the commitment of this intimate relationship give us the security we need to risk more of ourselves to achieve an even greater degree of closeness and intensity—of intimacy. Sex is an important means to that end, a physical expression of the trust and commitment between two people.

THE JUGGLING ACT

Establishing balance between these three elements —intimacy, security, and sex—used to be relatively easy. In fact, we almost did it by rote. Familiar scripts were handed down. Everybody had an assigned role. The lines were well rehearsed. In short, everyone knew the program. You got married; you settled down; husbands had jobs; wives had children. With this well-defined and socially prescribed division of labor, security was in the bag. Uprisings against the status quo were few and far between. Sex, too, for the better part of modern history, was rather strictly controlled by societal and moral dictates. Certain things were acceptable; certain things were not. The double standard flourished. And if, by some great fortune, you managed to escape the inhibitions of your upbringing enough to have a good sexual relationship with your partner, you certainly never bragged about it! Intimacy, too, was removed from the realm of reality. People got lost in the "hearts and flowers" romanticism of the songs, the romance novels, the movies—believing, in spite of their own dissatisfaction and loneliness, in the "happily ever after."

Somewhere in the sixties, all that began to change. We had what people quite rightly refer to as a "revolution." In fact, we had several of them! The liberation of men and women, both socially and sexually, has drastically changed the way the sexes relate to one another. With it, this liberation has brought new opportunities for relating, not just role-playing—opportunities for developing more in the areas of sex and intimacy without jeopardizing our personal security, our sense of balance as individuals. We are learning how to tolerate more insecurity than ever before, thanks to the support of a society that would have shrunk in horror at our new-found freedom, our crumbling role definitions, only twenty years ago.

It's a completely different ball game! Yet, when the going gets tough, we often fall back on the old rules, the old division of labor: The woman cooks and the man mows the lawn. But that's not all bad! This structure, this division, is just plain important to us for functioning. The difference is that, today, men and women have discovered that they have a choice about how these areas of responsibility should be divided. And that division should be responsive to the changing and evolving roles of each partner.

Sometimes these changes are drastic, for example, those caused by the growing number of women entering the work force. For the first time in the history of our country, about half of all women work outside the home. And that means incredible changes *inside* the home, in the realm previously ruled almost exclusively by the woman.

Some couples, like Ann and Jason, resist this change altogether. Ann and Jason are both professionals. Yet Jason takes no responsibility for the home and their four children, electing Ann chief cook and bottle washer by a vote of one (with one obviously overburdened, resentful, and silent abstainer). But instead of confronting Jason with the inequities of the situation, Ann holds tight to the security that these antiquated, irrelevant roles give her.

Others are trying to find new ways of working together as a couple. The man who feels that the home is the woman's job but still asks, "What can I do to help?" is making progress. But he's not quite there. If responsibilities are to be truly shared, we decide *together* how they will be divided. Similarly, the woman who works because she wants to, even though she still feels guilt over not being at home with her children, is also headed in the right direction. Both of these types of men and women are learning to balance the insecurity of shifting roles with the increased intimacy that comes from truly sharing in a relationship. They don't quite know how to handle these fluid roles with security. But they're working at it.

Betsy and Pete are such a couple. They waited for

ten years after their marriage, until both had their college teaching careers well established, to have their first baby. This little seven-pound girl required some very big changes in their lives. If both Pete and Betsy were to continue teaching, they were going to have to learn how to share in the household chores and the care of their new daughter. Betsy couldn't handle everything. First, they listed the chores and activities that needed to be done to keep their lives running smoothly. Then they sat and talked about what each of them liked or, more accurately, disliked least in each department. Finally, they divided everything up, except for the one chore both hated most—cleaning the bathroom. After a week of negotiations, no settlement could be reached. So they compromised and decided to take turns at the job. When it came to the baby, they felt that she was truly theirs, so dividing her care was no problem.

It all sounds so easy. But frankly, Betsy and Pete are the exception, not the rule. Far too many couples, even in the face of shifting social sanctions, are like Cal and Lorie. Both Cal and Lorie had worked or gone to school full time throughout their fourteen years of marriage. But never in all those years had they shared household responsibilities. Now, before you jump to conclusions about how unfair Cal was, let me say that it was Lorie who set up the "job descriptions." It was Lorie who felt that she could, and *should*, work *and* care for the house. After all, if Cal was understanding enough to *let* her work, the least she could do was keep a clean house and have a hot meal on the table every night.

Now, it should come as no real surprise that Cal had no quibble with Lorie's definitions! Since both partners agreed, in principle, you would think that there would be no problems. But Lorie resented working seven days a week, sixteen hours a day. And she was afraid to say anything to Cal directly. So she took it out on him in small ways, belittling him whenever possible, disparaging his work, falling prey to a "headache" whenever he approached her sexually. She sulked. She threw tantrums. But she never spoke up. Cal began to treat her like a child instead of a partner and an adult. Intimacy waned, and he became increasingly less interested in Lorie as a sexual partner. But everybody was nice and secure. Nobody was going anywhere, literally and figuratively.

Lorie illustrates a common plight for many women today that I think few people have noticed. I know of this plight from my lectures and discussions with women's groups in which the majority of women do not work outside the home. These are your young, middle-class women, like Lorie, who are usually well educated and have two or three children. They often respond with visible, open relief to my examples of women who have chosen homemaking and child rearing as their career. I was at first surprised that these women needed approval and permission to *not* be working wives and mothers. Then, in thinking it over, I became aware that social sanctions have changed so dramatically that most of our praise today is *not* for the "model mother" of the past who stayed home to raise her children but for the Supermom, the all-purpose career woman and homemaker. *She* is now the ideal, the complete and totally liberated woman. She appears on TV and in magazines and newspapers as a new, emerging, powerful role model—so powerful, in fact, that women are beginning to feel that they must defend their choice to work at home.

When I ask them the question, What do you do all day? these women become almost defensive. Only recently have they begun to see their home lives as careers. They are beginning to develop a true job description of homemaker and mother. They are beginning to recognize that they have a real choice. And it is a liberating experience for them.

These kinds of choices are not the exclusive purview of the female gender. I am often impressed with how young men, too, are welcoming their growing options. Bobby was an active proponent of equality when he married Sheila. Much to his chagrin, he found that Sheila had something quite different in mind. She wanted to be protected like a little Dresden doll. Having always had someone to take care of her, Sheila now expected Bobby to assume this caretaker role. But he would have none of it. To her plaintive "Oh, I can't cook, Bobby," he would reply, "If you want to eat every other night, you'll just have to learn." Bobby refused to treat Sheila like a child, to protect her as though she were too fragile to cope with the world. It took three years of constant juggling for Sheila to grow from an adolescent to an adult. In that time, she discovered that the rewards, in terms of intimacy, for being an adult far outweighed the security of being a child. Because of Bobby's stubborn refusal to accept her feelings of inadequacy, Sheila developed a sense of personal security that enabled her to turn loose of the traditional roles and to share life as an adult—intimately, sexually—with Bobby.

This social revolution has erased most of the pat formulas for relating, leaving each couple with the freedom and often the frustration of deriving its own. One other recent revolution has done a great deal to emancipate men and women from the roles that governed their relationships in the past: the sexual one. Almost single-handedly, this revolution's mightiest weapon, a small pill taken each morning, toppled the barriers to sexual involvement. That little pill freed women to discover more about sex, their own sexuality, and their own sexual desires and needs. And social acceptance of their new-found freedom also freed men to express their desires more openly, without fear of offense. And this freedom has done much to make sex a more enjoyable experience for both partners, for it encourages couples to work together for mutual pleasure, to be open and responsive to their own and each other's sexual needs, and to be willing to admit their ignorance and learn together.

But it has also affected the feeling of security for both sexes and impressed upon many couples the difficulties of the juggling act we have been talking about. Peggy and Thomas anticipated no difficulties whatsoever! Freedom beckoned, and they were eager to seize it. They even came to me for help. They wanted to improve their sexual relationship. They wanted some adventure. They were ready for some fun. Both had been divorced two years when they met, in their late thirties. Peggy was ready to shed all the bedroom roles she had inherited. Thomas, too, was eager to break out of the sexual patterns that had confined his marriage for twelve years. But in the areas of intimacy and security, both felt that they had plenty of experience. They just weren't concerned about those departments.

Now, my own assessment of their relationship was that both Thomas and Peggy, particularly Peggy, knew far less about intimacy, and hence security and insecurity, than they did about sex. But knowing how this juggling act usually works and how each of these elements is so closely tied together, I was more than willing to start with sex. Both Peggy and Thomas saw sex as a great learning adventure. Both could admit that they were ignorant in many areas and so were not as frightened or unsure. And both were open and receptive to each other's needs. They began by discussing those needs openly. "I like to take a shower together before we make love," Peggy would say. "All that silly splashing and fun is a nice prelude to sex."

And Thomas would respond, "I've never tried it! I've always taken sex so seriously! Laughter was never a part of it."

In turn, Thomas expressed his need for Peggy to show how much she enjoyed touching him. He had always felt that it was wrong for a man to need tenderness, so this request was a big step forward for him. Peggy was delighted. She enjoyed touching Thomas's body but had always felt that men preferred to be the ones to touch in a sexual way.

Their willingness as a couple to ask openly for what they wanted and to say no to what they did not want opened up a whole new world of sexual experience for Peggy and Thomas. Sex became a truly enjoyable experience, ever changing, ever unique. They willingly expressed their needs. They laughed. They played. They were tender. Behind their very own backs, they were becoming increasingly intimate. And when that fact began to dawn on them—that the other person was becoming very close, very central—the feelings of insecurity came flooding in. Although she enjoyed sharing sexually, Peggy began to express a wish that they spend less time together, that they pursue outside interests with friends. She was getting scared. She wanted to withdraw from the relationship. Thomas was becoming too important. She backed off, blaming Thomas for their inability to pursue the relationship further. There were problems, she said. Thomas's children. His job change. All the pressures on him.

In truth, Thomas had been asking Peggy to share some of these problems with him, to discuss his fears and anxieties. But Peggy wanted him to be strong, not anxious. She wanted him to be a "man," to handle it. But she did not tell Thomas that his openness about his thoughts and feelings distressed her. She, instead, listened to his problems, told him how to solve them, and then became resentful when he did not follow her suggestions. She experienced his problems as a burden because she was trying to solve them rather than share them.

Thomas, too, was resentful. He felt that Peggy was trying to run his life, telling him how to treat his daughters, how to handle job problems. She was not listening to him. She was just spouting solutions. He felt used and manipulated. But he was afraid to tell Peggy. The honesty, he feared, would jeopardize their already faltering security. Neither Thomas nor Peggy knew how to correct the problem, how to share and be intimate. Fearful of the pain that their separation, even at this point, would cause, they reined in hard on their sexual sharing as well. Their total relationship came to a standstill.

Before it started sliding backward, I helped Thomas and Peggy understand that, just as admitting their mutual ignorance in the area of sex had freed them to begin learning together, accepting that neither of them knew as much about intimacy as they thought they did would also give them the security they needed to begin developing in this area. With this admission of ignorance and a trust in their ability to learn, Peggy and Thomas were able to open up to one another again. Thomas was able to say, "I want to share my problems with you. I am not asking you to solve them for me. In fact, I don't want you to give me any answers or suggestions. I just want you to share my feelings. I will come up with my own answers." And Peggy replied, "What a relief! I thought that sharing your problems meant that I needed to care enough to *solve* them for you!"

Peggy and Thomas learned a lot about juggling. They learned that you can't tinker with any one of these basic needs without shifting the others as well. The ability to balance these basic needs, like all the other essential abilities in building a relationship, requires work to cultivate. There is a starting point somewhere, where we either will not or cannot juggle at all. We then, with a little practice, become a novice juggler, then a good one, then a professional one. But none of us ever reach the point where we do not drop one of the balls once in a while.

This ability enables us to make adjustments, to maintain balance as our needs for security, for intimacy, for sex fluctuate. There are many levels of each. And sometimes we need far more, or less, of one than of another. In a relationship that is alive, growing, and developing, those levels deepen. As we work toward more intimacy, our sharing and caring for our partner enhances trust and commitment. Hence, we feel more secure, freer to risk ourselves further, sexually and emotionally. As we work to improve our sexual relationship, we become more secure in our knowledge of one another's needs and desires and so can risk more in the other arenas. And, as we work on the trust and honesty that are the foundation of the only *real* security in a marriage, we become increasingly intimate with one another.

In learning to balance these needs, we discover the secret that those who have mastered this juggling routine have known all along. We discover that we don't have to give up one thing for another, that we don't have to make trade-offs. We discover that what were once three apparently separate elements—security, intimacy, and sex—become inseparable, melding into an integrated, complete whole. We have a relationship. We have a marriage. We discover, in short, that we can have it all.

4

How to Ruin a Perfectly Good Marriage

You've worked hard to get here. You've been through the sharing and the caring. You've discovered the intensity. You've made the commitment. You've established a balance between the intimacy and the security you need from your partner. And you've learned that love is more than "making love"—though you've learned a lot about that too.

You have a friend as well as a lover. You have that sense of real closeness, of belonging, with another human being. You have a thing of meaning. You have a marriage.

And you expect to have it for the rest of your life. Everybody does. Rarely does an individual make, or accept, this commitment with the thought that it might, even just *might*, not work out. Rarely is there a serious question that there will be anything but a "happily ever after" ending. After all, that is what we promise each other: to live by the rules, to try very hard, to be very careful, to stick together for better or worse.

All well-intentioned, all loving thoughts and goals. So where are all these unhappy endings coming from? How do we systematically, though often unknowingly, go about undermining what we have so painstakingly and lovingly built? Where does this feeling come from that the harder we try, the less we seem to have? the tighter we hold, the more we seem to lose? the more careful we are, the more we seem to destroy? What is happening? Like the raccoon carefully washing his precious sugar cube in the stream, we clasp our relationship tightly and watch, in astonishment and disappointment, as it dissolves before us.

It's like a cruel joke, a bitter "Catch 22," because we're *trying!* We're trying all the techniques, playing by all the rules we were told would work, believed would work, would keep us—and our relationship—safe.

No one stopped to explain that that was quite impossible. *No* relationship is safe, unless it is dead. The more alive and vital it is, the more is at risk. The more intimate and sexual, the less secure. The richer, the more we stand to lose. So what do we do? Almost instinctively, we do everything in our power to diminish the risk, to increase our security, to preserve our relationship, and, ultimately, to diminish and destroy it. The processes may be innocent, even unconscious. But they can be devastating.

PROTECTING

You have something valuable. You have a relationship with someone you love and feel close to. It's far too important to lose. So you're careful. You don't take chances. You try very hard not to hurt your partner or yourself or the marriage. You call it all sorts of things: settling down, being considerate, compromising. But it all boils down to protecting—not just the marriage but ourselves. Like an overprotective parent, we coddle our marriage, bundle it up, suffocate it. We do it not out of malice or of cruelty but truly out of a desire to please, to nurture, to love. We don't want to hurt anyone—not our partner, not ourselves.

Melanie knew that she hurt Jess with her excuses—a headache, problems with the children, a fight with a friend—to avoid sex. But she feared that the truth would hurt him more. She could not enjoy sex unless she felt close to him. And after thirteen years of marriage, those times were few and far between. So, as far as sex was concerned, Melanie could take it or leave it and usually preferred to leave it. Jess did not understand Melanie's need and was only aware that sex was a dull and hurried affair. In not wanting to hurt Jess's feelings, and risk having to pay any unpleasant consequences, Melanie was unwilling to be open about her needs. She believed that she was protecting Jess. She was protecting herself. And she was ruining their relationship.

As we systematically eliminate talking about and dealing with these areas that are most vital to us, we cut off all the new shoots, the areas of growth. We prune our relationship back until it is a dry, lifeless, brittle stump.

It's so tempting to do. "Just this one time," we tell ourselves. "I'll tell him [her] tomorrow," we lie. "It's no big deal," we say unconvincingly. We use a hundred little excuses to avoid conflict, risk, potential hurt, and loss.

You know the ones:

"I'll bring up the subject [any "touchy" one will do nicely] when he's in a better mood."

"She'd be hurt if she knew how I *really* feel about this [be it how she squeezes the toothpaste tube or approaches sex], so it's better left unsaid."

"I'm too tired to discuss it tonight. I'll bring it up this weekend [or, if friends drop in, next Wednesday—when you can tell yourself that it wasn't very important anyway]."

"He'll be furious if I tell him what happened [whether you overspent the budget or used his best golf shirt as a dust cloth by mistake], so I'll just let it go and hope he doesn't find out."

"She has been so cold and distant lately. But if I wait long enough, she's bound to change, and things [from dinner conversation to sex] will be all right again."

Sound familiar? All of us, at one time or another, have used such excuses to postpone or sidestep those areas of potential pain or confrontation in our relationship.

But these little deceptions have a way of perpetuating themselves until the gulf between us and truth, if we can still recognize it, is almost unbridgeable. So we protect ourselves even more. It takes courage to break this chain, this momentum. But the longer it goes on, the higher the price.

Melanie found that courage only when her estrangement from Jess became intolerably painful. Melanie and Jess had protected their relationship so long that they had lost each other in the mirage of a happy marriage. They had never honestly shared their feelings about their life together. Oh, they talked about his work or her students or their children. They even talked, sometimes, about their feelings toward each other. But it was always positive, *very* positive—except, that is, for those times when Melanie would fly into an uncontrolled rage and say or do anything to hurt Jess. At those times Jess felt overwhelmed by her anger.

And Melanie felt guilty and contrite. So she would try to make up with Jess, and he, feeling quite the martyr, would forgive her. An uneasy peace would reign until the next flare-up, while unresolved problems, resentments, and hurts continued to smolder in the growing distance between them.

Melanie had to do something. She began by tackling just one of the problems in her relationship with Jess: her growing sense of physical isolation. The only place to begin was with the truth. She never felt that Jess saw her as attractive or desirable. She never felt that he wanted to touch her just to be close. At first Jess was threatened and confused by her feelings because he *did* find Melanie beautiful and often wanted just to feel her close to him. But he tried to understand her feelings and discover why she was not getting this message from him.

What Jess discovered was that Melanie needed the *words* from him, not just the actions. She needed to hear him say, "You look so pretty today," or, "I love the way you smell when you get out of the bath," or, "Touching you feels so good." As Jess began to understand Melanie's needs, he learned to give and express his feelings for her in a way she could understand. And Melanie did the same.

In telling each other what they wanted and needed, they began to know each other in a new and fresh way. Today, six years later, this freshness prevails, as Melanie and Jess continue to be open and honest about their feelings toward each other.

Protecting almost ruined this marriage. Melanie and Jess learned the hard way that while this process—this deliberate, methodical cover-up of negative feelings—may work for a while, it is usually only a stalling measure, postponing the inevitable confrontation with the truth. They learned, too, that protecting works just as effectively on the little things (like making beds) as on the big things (like making love), providing fuel for resentment, guilt, loneliness.

Thwarting this process requires that we settle the score, air our feelings, with our partner daily, even if that means some minor skirmishing.

Conflict—fighting, if you will—is essential to flush out and meet the needs of both parties in a marriage. Men often tell me, "I want to be comfortable in this marriage, to feel safe, to feel that my wife is loyal to me." Women, while sharing many of these needs, often say, "I want excitement in this relationship, something happening." We often battle over these opposites, thinking that it is a choice between the two. But in a good relationship, there is time and room for both needs. In fact, the ebb and flow of the two is essential for both stability and growth. Just as a life without stress is boring, so a relationship without this tension, this push and pull, is stifling. This stress, these problems and disagreements, are necessary in a marriage, for they foster growth and change. But too much stress, or continued stress, within an individual or in a relationship is crippling.

To shrink from fighting is to protect. To protect is to contribute to the slow, boring decay of a relationship. Fighting is a sign of life, of working. It is a healthy sign that there is something going on between two people. Unfortunately, we often feel that the price of fighting is too high: hurt feelings, anger, even perhaps a night alone on the couch. But the price of continual peace, pleasantness, politeness is much higher.

After fourteen years Glenda and Joe had virtually destroyed their marriage by keeping it calm and peaceful at all costs. Apathy reigned. But Joe was bored. He wanted more excitement in their relationship. He wanted to feel closer to Glenda. So he began to rock the boat, to demand more from her. He began by approaching Glenda one step at a time, first by getting in touch with what he wanted and then asking for it in a direct, honest, open way. One thing he wanted was a more open acknowledgment of affection. But Glenda literally did not know what he wanted when he demanded more closeness.

"Glenda," he said, "it would really mean a lot to me if you would greet me with a hug when I come home. I need to be touched. It makes me feel loved."

"Joe," she responded, "you know that I'm not physically demonstrative. And, besides, I'm in the midst of cooking dinner when you come in."

"But I'm not happy with so little physical touching," Joe persisted.

"All right, I'll give it a try," Glenda conceded. "But my heart won't be in it."

"Of course it won't be at first," Joe said. "But I'm willing to see if it can develop into something we both enjoy."

So, with this simple step, they began. And it worked. Glenda began to realize how much she got from touching for a moment, and Joe began to share more with Glenda in return. They then added talking together for thirty minutes when Joe first got home to share their feelings about the day. Each part they added enhanced the intensity they felt in the relationship. Their first real argument caused them much pain. They felt isolated from each other. They felt hurt. They felt lonely and eager to be back together with a renewed sense of closeness.

This interplay of pleasure, pain, isolation, and closeness infuses the relationship with intensity. It was the willingness to go for broke, to quit protecting, that changed Glenda and Joe's marriage from a charade into a vital force. Beginning with the simple words, "I need you," Joe began to open up their relationship by showing his feelings honestly and demanding the same from Glenda.

Sometimes the risk is great. In wanting to be close,

we may quit protecting only to find that our partner cannot satisfy that wanting. Jamie and Ross look like the perfect couple. Ross is a highly successful professional and Jamie, an attractive, intelligent woman active in community affairs and volunteer work. After twelve years of marriage, they look as if they have made it. They live in a beautiful home in the right neighborhood, have the right friends, belong to the right tennis club, and send their two children to the right private school.

But Ross is depressed and feels that everything is a burden. Jamie, on the other hand, goes glibly about her days like a mechanical doll that is wound up each morning. When I asked Ross, "What do you want from a marriage?" he gave me all the right answers: "I want to share life with someone. I want to see my wife as my best friend. I want sex to be a part of feeling close, not just something we do together—like playing tennis. I want to share myself, to feel that my good points are appreciated and my limitations accepted. I want to feel that my wife is the most special woman in the world."

Ross has wanted, has tried, to achieve such a relationship with Jamie for years. But suddenly, as he really examined his list of wants, he realized something: "It is not Jamie that I want these things from. It is a 'someone,' a person." Ross saw Jamie as devoid of feelings, a caricature of a person. "I don't want anything from her but a divorce," Ross finally acknowledged. "I cannot be intimate with her because I do not really want to be close to her. I do not 'want' from her." That left him with two options: to live with a dead relationship or to divorce.

In his twelve years of marriage to Jamie, Ross had gone far beyond protecting their relationship—far beyond hiding his feelings of resentment, longing, loneliness. He had gone to the point where he could actually convince himself, could pretend, that those feelings did not exist.

PRETENDING

Pretending often goes hand in hand with protecting. But it takes cover-up one step further: out of the realm of the conscious and deliberate into the realm, ultimately, of the unconscious. Pretending means not only sweeping any threatening truths or feelings under the carpet or into the closet but denying that they exist at all. After all, they weren't in the fairy tales or the movie scripts or the novels. So they couldn't possibly be part of marriage, could they? If we just assume our proper roles, we tell ourselves, everything will go according to the program. Pretending is something we all mastered as children, developing elaborate fantasies about cowboys and Indians, princesses and prince charmings, bogeymen and invisible playmates. We knew it was only make-believe. But it was fun. As adults, such games still play an important part in our lives—in sex, in creativity, in just plain fun.

During their first struggling year of marriage, Lisa and Scott would pretend, on their weekly adventure at the grocery store, that money was no object. They would pretend that the only reason they were not buying steak was that they did not *like* steak. They pretended that they far preferred hamburger six nights a week and chicken on Sunday. They weren't really fooling anybody, least of all themselves, about what was and what wasn't. And what *wasn't* was money. But the pretending made that fact a little easier to accept.

Pretending can add a positive dimension to our lives, as long as we *know* we are pretending. It only becomes destructive when we are not honest about it, with ourselves or with others. We harbor our illusions, assume our roles, rehearse our scripts. In short, we construct a make-believe world and don't even realize what we have done.

Like Marilyn. Fresh out of college, she married Dick only three months after they met. It was time. They wanted to be married. Dick wanted a wife. Marilyn wanted a husband. But she also wanted a few extra things, like a career. Unfortunately, that wasn't in the particular script that Marilyn inherited, and having it required a lot of extra work. So, the wife arose at five o'clock to cook a big breakfast for the husband before they both went to work. And with some of their income, they bought a washer and dryer so the wife wouldn't have to go to the Laundromat after dark. Sometimes the wife threw private tantrums as she collected her husband's dirty socks to put in their new washer and dryer in their big new house. One day she picked up a shoe to slam on the floor in anger and slammed it into her thigh instead.

Even with a nasty bruise on her leg, Marilyn never really stopped to listen. This was simply the way it was. And the way it was, she told herself and all those around her, was happy. She almost convinced herself. It might have worked, too, if a shred of truth had not crept in one day when she stepped off a plane after a week-long business trip to be greeted by a man she didn't know, and didn't love, who was her husband. That sharp encounter with reality jolted Marilyn out of her make-believe world. She could no longer pretend that this was the way it should be at all. Within three weeks they separated, and three months later they divorced.

Sometimes, if we cannot kid ourselves, kidding those around us is the next best thing. Tim would have had a pretty tough time pretending to himself that he was not having an affair. It was his wife, Carrie, he had to convince. For over a year, Carrie had felt that something was wrong. Tim was always tired. He worked late. He spent weekends at the office. When she asked why, he would always explain, "I have to work this hard to earn the kind of money we need. As soon as I make partner, I can slow down." Then he would add apologetically, "I know I don't have much time for you and the children now. But you know I love you. That's why I'm working so hard."

Tim pretended to Carrie that all was well—that he was always late coming home because he had to work, that he was not interested in sex because he was so overworked. He pretended that there was no problem. And so did Carrie. She knew deep inside that Tim was having an affair. The evidence was overwhelming. But she pretended, both to herself and to him, that it was not true. It would hurt too much to face it.

Ultimately, this charade began to take its toll. Tim began to develop signs of physical distress. After a thorough checkup his doctor pegged tension as the major culprit and explained that the repercussions could be serious if Tim did not resolve whatever problems were producing this inordinate stress.

During our second visit Tim told me of his affair. He fully realized that his guilt over his double life was the cause of his distress. After examining what he most valued in his life, Tim chose to tell his mistress good-by and to work on the relationship with Carrie.

But when I suggested that he tell Carrie the truth about the affair, he adamantly refused. I explained that I could not become a partner in his pretense. To do this would only help perpetuate his world of make-believe. Tim had not been loving or caring toward Carrie for more than a year. He finally chose to tell her the truth about that year. Then the real work on the relationship began. There were many times that

Carrie's anger and hurt made Tim wish that he had never confided in her. There were also many times that Carrie wished the same thing because she could no longer pretend that they had the ideal marriage. The truth, that together they had lived a life of sham for at least four solid years, was indeed painful. They had lost a lot of ground. But it was important for Tim and Carrie to recognize that, to see clearly what *was*, and to begin to rebuild from that point.

It took six months of intense work on the part of each even to begin that rebuilding process. But that work enabled Tim and Carrie to develop a relationship based on complete honesty and real trust, not on pretense.

The insidious thing about pretending is that the illusion often *becomes* the reality. Like Candide, we cannot see beyond "whatever is is right." We deny the truth—the strengths and limitations—of ourselves, our spouses, our marriages. So we cannot see what areas we need to work on to improve.

If a relationship is to have real substance, we must be open to see and be seen completely—just as we are. And we must respond honestly to what we see in each other and in our relationship. Our responses, our feelings, will not always be positive. But if we cannot feel the bad feelings without feeling despair, we begin to build illusions. We fool ourselves about the relationship and become more and more isolated and unable to truly be with people, much less involved in the relationship. This is what Paula refers to when she speaks of her journey to never-never land.

Twenty years of marriage had gradually transformed Paula from an outgoing, vital person into a quiet, brooding recluse. She retreated into child rearing and reading, hiding from her own awareness of the emptiness of her relationship with her husband. She literally refused to look at the lack of communication between her and her husband, Randy; the lack of sexual interest; the lack of sharing, of caring, of intimacy; the lack, even, of wanting those things.

Paula lived in a never-never land, where pretense passed for reality, where community activities passed for sharing, where children passed for caring and love. Then Randy had an affair. Paula had been so busy pretending for twenty years that she was truly shocked to discover that anything was awry. That jolt brought her crashing back to earth. She put her book down, put the children in the back seat, and looked.

What she saw was that there was nothing, absolutely nothing, happening between her and Randy. There was no substance to their relationship. Paula couldn't pretend anymore. She couldn't pretend that she and Randy had the perfect marriage, that she wasn't hurt, that she didn't have feelings. She couldn't go back. And she was determined to go forward, with or without Randy.

Once Paula vented her anger and frustration openly, they could begin to work on the cause. But progress was slow. Randy was reluctant. "You will never be satisfied, no matter what I do," he would respond to Paula's demands. "You could at least give me credit for how hard I am trying."

And try he did—to go back to pretending that nothing was wrong, and to convince Paula of it. He would arrange exotic vacations and romantic weekend getaways and then expect Paula to pretend that everything was just perfect. When she refused to go along with the game, he would adopt his loving martyr role.

A constant battle raged inside Paula between the idyllic calm of that make-believe world and the turmoil of a real life in which she had a relationship of value. It would have been easier in the short run for Paula to go along with Randy, to pretend that everything was as it should be. But in the long run, they would have purchased their tickets back to never-never land. And the road out is not an easy one.

If we're lucky, like Paula and Randy, we journey out of that nether world to build a real, solid relationship with our spouse. Sometimes, like Evelyn, we fight our way back only to find that there is nothing solid on which to build.

When I met Evelyn, she was drinking—heavily, silently, slyly—because she could no longer pretend that her life was even bearable without the help of alcohol. For years her husband had protected her, pretending that nothing was wrong—that Evelyn was simply tired, not drunk.

Before either she or I could discover what she was trying to hide from herself by drinking, we had to get her sober. Her life was a shambles. And she first had to rebuild her own world before she could even look at the one she shared with her husband. Once Evelyn quit drinking, she became aware of the hard, cold truth (and that almost drove her back to her bottle): She did not love her husband. In fact, she found him dull and stupid. She realized that she had married him those many, many years ago out of dependency, not love. Evelyn finally—after eighteen years and three children—quit pretending to feel emotions she did not have. She divorced her husband and has not remarried in the ensuing five years. In that time she has built a new life on what is real, not make-believe. She is just beginning to establish a relationship with a man who shares many of her interests. And this time Evelyn is determined not to pretend about what is important to her. She knows that, for her, it is a life-and-death matter. She knows that to pretend again would drive her back to drinking, which, to her, is a living death.

While the outcomes appear very different on the

surface, both Paula and Evelyn got the same thing. Both would not give an inch in terms of their commitment to living with honesty, first with themselves and then with their spouses. They refused to go back. They refused to pretend, to be confined by the roles and illusions that defined their lives and their relationships.

Coping with, and ultimately burying, the personal illusions that each and every one of us carries into marriage would be difficult enough without society's undying efforts to preserve them. Sexual candor often passes for honesty in a relationship. But the real "secrets" of marriage—what it gives and what it takes—are known only to the initiated. Yet at each new initiation ceremony, each wedding, these secrets are carefully guarded, cloaked in the illusion that for *this* couple, marriage will be romantic, blissful, eternal.

Now when (not *if!*) you discover that such is not the case, you are more than slightly encouraged to keep that little truth to yourself. Things are expected now—certain things of the husband, certain things of the wife. And despite the strides made in the last several years, we, along with society, expect these things of ourselves. Hard as we may fight it, these roles come with the script, and, while they make day-to-day existence easier, they make *living* impossible.

These roles provide great excuses for not getting involved with our partner. The man who works seventy hours a week can hide behind his righteousness, saying to his wife and children, "I am doing this for you. I've given my all at the office. You can't ask anything more of me." Our puritan ethic has sanctioned, if not downright endorsed, this attitude. The price is incredibly high for those who try to be involved with this shell of a man. A couple I once counseled lived a life of misery for forty years. Now the executive vice-president of a large oil company, the man is much admired and respected for his multiple accomplishments. When he and his wife were forty-five, his wife begged him to spend more time with, to be closer to, her and the children. His inevitable response was, "I want to, but you know I can't help it if my job requires so much of me."

His two sons were unable to find their place in life. The oldest committed suicide. The youngest required intensive psychiatric care. Yet the father felt no responsibility for what happened to his sons. Instead he blamed their mother for improper care. She in turn became so depressed that she was unable to function.

Women, too, find escape in their roles, spending from dawn to dusk immersed in motherhood. These women come in two basic varieties: Sneaker Mom and Wonder Mother. Tennis shoes and a station wagon are the hallmarks of the Sneaker Mom, no matter what the time of day. She spends most of her time shuttling children to Little League practice, piano lessons, or scout meetings. Dinner means Big Macs or Kentucky Fried Chicken because she is too busy with her children's activities to bother with cooking. When her husband arrives home, Sneaker Mom is too exhausted to do much but take her tennis shoes off and watch TV. She's hiding from herself and her spouse, pretending that the demands of children are so overwhelming that she has nothing left over for anything else.

Now Wonder Mother is a much more polished pretender—quite perfect, in fact. She is up at dawn, hair in place, mascara on, cooking a balanced breakfast for her family. The house is spotless each day by noon. And in the afternoon she serves as PTA chairperson, den mother, or band booster president. But she's always home by four o'clock to supervise the children and cook another wholesome meal. In contrast to the husband of Sneaker Mom, the Wonder Mother's costar is always greeted with a perfunctory kiss from a perfectly attired wife who is too busy with the children to really notice him.

These overzealous mothers are not products of my imagination. They are real. You see them all the time —in supermarkets and at Little League games. They're the wives with the husbands who also want to pretend that life is wonderful, as they smile at each other over the kids sandwiched between them.

These men and women are the self-righteous individuals. "I have been working so hard," they say. "What more do you expect from me?" As if work, or children, excused us from being close to those we love!

We hide behind our roles, wrap ourselves in our illusions. Pretense becomes our reality. We do not see ourselves, our spouse, or the relationships clearly. And without this clear understanding and recognition of what is, and what *isn't,* in a relationship, we cannot even tell where we stand, let alone where we are going. That is the first step. We must look honestly at where we stand in the relationship and accept the reality of what we have—good or bad, more or less. But that is not enough. To stop short at acceptance is sure death for the relationship.

After twenty-five years of marriage, Jean knew what she and Gary had. And it wasn't bad, exactly. It was just "less"—less than Jean knew she wanted and needed. But she accepted her lot and her relationship with Gary. After all, she told herself, he was a good man—well-intentioned, if not particularly affectionate; a strong father, if not a particularly loving husband. In the evenings Gary always put down his paper and pretended to listen to Jean when she tried to engage him in conversation. It scarcely mattered whether she was talking about a new novel she had read recently or a truly serious problem with one of their children.

Gary always nodded and said, "That's interesting," or, "Is that right?" Seldom was there any further discussion. But Jean accepted that and watched TV or talked with friends on the telephone until bedtime.

On the rare occasions when they had sex (not made love), Gary would perfunctorily touch Jean but never kiss or caress her lovingly, passionately. Afterward he would immediately fall asleep while Jean lay beside him with unshed tears, feeling desolate and alone. But she accepted that too. And always the next morning, she would cook Gary's breakfast and lovingly send him off to work. Jean accepted. She pretended in the light of day that life was good, that she needed nothing—indeed, *wanted* nothing—but to fill her time with shopping, housekeeping, children, and friends. Only in the dark of night, and then only for a few moments, did she quit pretending and let the feelings of loneliness and emptiness come to her. But these she pushed quickly away. She never told Gary what she needed or of her times of crying. She lived, instead, with a feeling of quiet desperation, pretending and denying her own needs.

It was only when Jean bumped into something that she simply couldn't accept, Gary's three-year affair, that she quit pretending and started demanding the closeness and intimacy that she needed. Now that Gary has acknowledged his own need for closeness and begun to let Jean be with him, both are very much aware of the emptiness, the death, of those many years together. Jean refuses to go back. And so does Gary. They refuse to pretend anymore, to accept that it is enough to simply go through the motions of living.

Accepting the unacceptable. Tolerating the absolutely intolerable. Pretending that you have "enough," when you know darn good and well you don't! These are surefire ways to ruin a perfectly good marriage.

Certainly, we have no place to work from in our relationship other than where we are at this point in time. But that point should be looked at as a starting point, not the finish line. The critical step is to define what you want and need from your relationship that you are not currently getting. Then the real working begins. Down must come that last illusion that everything will happen automatically; that now that you're married, the relationship is solid, locked in, safe; that now you can put your feet up, breathe easier, take a few things for granted. After all, we persist in believing that loving someone just happens—easily, naturally.

LOAFING

This almost cultural illusion with which we are raised does not die easily. Yet it is this naive, hopeful, lovely illusion—that love makes everything else easy —that slowly but surely, day by ever more tedious lifeless day, will permit a once vital, healthy relationship to wither, to dry up.

Pattie and Richard once had such a relationship. Pattie had protected her first marriage into an early grave. So, determined not to make a second mistake, she lived with Richard for over a year before they married. During that year, they worked as a team on problems that arose in their relationship. They perceived problems, both their causes and their solutions, as mutual. They loved each other. And they devoted a lot of precious time and work and understanding to nurturing that love.

Now with all this sharing and caring and commitment and work you would think that if any couple was destined to live happily ever after, it would be Pattie and Richard. Not true. For the marriage turned out to be the beginning not of the beginning but of the end. As soon as they were married, Pattie and Richard each shouldered one of the deadly weapons in ruining their relationship. Richard took a new, more important and exciting job, which demanded much more of his time. But that was all right, he figured, because now that he and Pattie were married, she wouldn't require as much attention. His stated attitude was, "Now that we're married, I can begin to concentrate on my career." This statement, translated, meant "Finally, I can take a few things for granted!" So he began to put in all the work at the office, and none at home. His long hours left very little energy to devote to his relationship with Pattie.

Meanwhile, back on the home front, Pattie began accepting and accepting. She knew too much to pretend that everything was even passable, let alone perfect. But she could only muster the courage to demand more closeness about once every six months or so. And then it always came out in a whining, complaining way. Richard would respond to her demands with an indulgent "Of course, dear," topped off with dinner and a movie. He had discovered that that was the minimum he could get away with to keep Pattie happy—or, more correctly, keep her unhappiness at bay.

That does not mean that Richard did not love Pattie. He did, intensely. But he did not know how to be *loving*. Instead of talking to her, he bought her a new house. Instead of holding her, he bought her a new car.

Pattie, on the other hand, was so afraid of ruining a second marriage that she became even more protective of their relationship. She never got angry or demanded the closeness she so desperately wanted. After four years she and Richard were left with only the shell, the outer trappings, of marriage. Within that shell the relationship was lifeless.

Ultimately it was Pattie who could not tolerate, accept, the emptiness. One day she demanded that Richard take a day off and join her on a picnic. He reluctantly agreed, for it meant canceling a golf game with some important clients. On the drive to the park, he was moody. He complained about the heat, the inconvenience, the work he wasn't getting done. When they finally spread their picnic blanket, Richard was so busy reading some papers from the office that he could not be involved in sharing the afternoon with Pattie. That was the last straw! On the way home Pattie announced that she wanted out. She was no longer afraid to speak the truth. They shared nothing. They had nothing in common. She was alone and lonely. It was too late to salvage anything, and she knew it. Richard was devastated and begged her to stay. But, by this time, Pattie had no need to protect, for there was so little left of their relationship that it barely hurt to walk away.

What Pattie and Richard failed to realize is that a relationship requires care, nurturing, and attention to flourish. It takes work. You plant seeds; they become delicate green shoots. You water; those shoots become golden shafts of wheat. You harvest; that wheat becomes your bread, something to eat that gives you sustenance.

Here I must emphasize a very important distinction. I am not saying that to love someone is work. Feelings of wanting to be with someone, wanting to be part of their lives, are natural and spontaneous and take no effort. Such feelings are the essential ingredient of any loving relationship. They are the roots, the foundation, of a marriage. And Richard and Pattie had them. It is not this love, but rather *loving* someone, that is the work. We can perform loving acts without love. But we can also love and not know how to be loving.

Loving someone, as I mentioned earlier, involves both feeling and expression. First, we must *feel* love for another. Then we must *express* our love in such a way that the other person can experience it. That's where the work comes in. Before we can express our love appropriately, we must get to know the other person—what he or she needs, what makes him or her feel loved. And it means not being afraid to ask just what that is if necessary! Only in this way can we learn how to be loving, for what we may think is loving may not be experienced as such by the one we love.

After twenty-five years of marriage, the love that Leigh and Paul still feel for each other is unmistakable. Paul still loves Leigh in a way a young man of twenty loves his first girl. He would rather be with her than with anyone else and is strongly attracted to her sexually. Leigh feels the same way about Paul. As she says, "When I look up and see him across a room, my eyes just light up." So they've got the basic ingredient. But the problem is, neither feels or experiences the other's love. Leigh will say, "If he loved me, he would hear me when I tell him what I don't like. After all these years, he still does not love me enough to let me sleep late on Saturday, when he knows how much it means to me." Paul says, "If she loved me, she would not make fun of my faults. She wouldn't put me down so often."

Paul and Leigh are only now beginning to learn how to be loving toward each other. They first had to admit, "We love each other, but we do not know how to be loving." Slowly they are learning how to express their love for one another so that each can experience it and understand it. Learning begins by asking what is important to your partner, what makes your partner feel loved. Then you must start doing your best to express your love in that particular way. Elaborate expressions aren't always necessary. Sometimes the expression of love is very simple: Paul now makes sure that Leigh can sleep late on Saturday. Sometimes it is more complex: Paul and Leigh are now learning to express their love sexually in a way that brings more satisfaction to both.

It's not always easy. Leigh is not crazy about all of Paul's interests—like baseball. But she loves him, so she takes up people-watching at Saturday games so that they can share the time together. The feeling of love is natural. The act of loving is work. That is where the distinction comes. It's simple but important. We cannot work to gain the feeling of love for someone. We can work at expressing that natural feeling in a loving way, in a way our partner can understand.

Now this "work" doesn't mean sitting quietly and logically figuring out what the problems in a relationship are. We can't truly work on a relationship when we're being rational and objective. We can only work on it when we are involved—when our feelings, our guts as well as our heads, are in there working. Sometimes that involvement means yelling and shouting, fighting toe to toe to come up with a solution. But even then the love finds expression. During a knock-down-drag-out fight with her husband, Skip, over how to handle a problem with their son, Sandy let a grin slip out. Skip couldn't help but smile and say, "I love you." And in that moment all the work became joyously rewarding.

Now I am not saying that this involvement, this work, requires problem solving all the time. It doesn't. Over half the time should be spent on being together, sharing day-to-day activities and feelings. And some of the time must be spent apart. We need the whole range of feelings, from tenderness to anger, to be truly involved with a partner.

The work comes daily in expressing and sharing those feelings honestly. And that takes the commitment of both partners. But first it requires an acknowledgment that you need this involvement.

It took Roger thirteen years of marriage to Diana to recognize that need. Roger created a vivid image to describe those years for me. He saw himself alone in a tall, peaceful tower. Diana stood below and called to him, "Come join me. Come share with me!" He called back, "Why should I? Why should I give up this peace and quiet for the stress, the pain, the arguments? I'll just stay here, thank you, where I am in complete control of what happens to me."

But, increasingly, Roger felt that he was missing something—something he saw that others had. That was pleasure, not just pain. He had to admit that he wanted it. And then he had to admit that he had no idea of how to get it. But he began working, in the simplest way, by telling Diana about his day and asking about hers. At first the conversation was extremely stilted, like a first-grader's "show and tell." But soon Roger discovered that he enjoyed telling Diana of his life—his dreams, his heartaches. He enjoyed listening to her. He enjoyed the sharing. The "practice" was at last becoming pleasure. He felt less isolated, less depressed. Each week he added something new—something that would help him move closer to Diana, like sharing household chores. Although Diana worked outside the home, she had always done these tasks alone—angrily, but alone. As Roger began to share the responsibilities of running a home, he found that he liked Diana more without her angry, martyr role. Diana, in turn, felt more cared for and hence more caring toward Roger.

Now here is where the give-and-take comes in, for Diana had gotten a lot of mileage out of that martyr role—"I'm so overburdened. Life is so much work."

It was hard to give it up. She was losing her old, valued position because Roger was beginning to share, to demand to be closer to her. That made it increasingly difficult for her to hide behind the overburdened housewife–working woman role. So in one phase of Roger's changing, she decided that she wasn't sure that she wanted him to change and actually began to sabotage his efforts. But by this time Roger felt so good about being more involved with Diana that he just forged ahead until she realized that it might be to her advantage to cooperate, to change too.

This refusing to give up, this willingness to support the other, shifts from one partner to the other as the relationship develops, just as it did for Diana and Roger. If one gives up, the other doesn't. If one gets tired and discouraged, the other keeps working. Without this give-and-take, it's difficult to maintain the intensity. No one can keep it going alone.

It is this going back and forth that produces change, that keeps a relationship alive. It's painful sometimes. We may even have to give up things, like Diana did her martyr role, that have paid some dividends. But change in one partner demands change in the other. That is what makes the relationship a dynamic, vital process.

RESISTING CHANGE

Change is frightening, to be sure. There are no guarantees on the outcome, no assurances that both partners will change together or will even want each other when the process is complete. But when one partner, or both, tries to protect the relationship by resisting this change, growth is stunted. This is where commitment comes in. Again, we are not talking about the all-or-nothing, forever-and-ever variety. We are talking about the commitment to ourselves and to the

relationship *for this day;* the commitment to encourage our partner to change and grow as he or she
must; the commitment to work to understand, to love,
and to be with that changing person.

Change is the constant in any relationship. It is
inevitable, necessary. And it *will* occur, for good or
bad, no matter what you do. Resistance itself is action
and will produce a response, a change, in the other
person. You can't fight it. So the key is to recognize
change, welcome it, and grow from it. As individuals
grow and develop, they, of necessity, change. The same
is true of our society. Its swings from conservative
to liberal, lenient to strict, self-centered to humani-
tarian will inevitably precipitate change in the individual and, hence, in the relationship.

One of these swings that very directly affects the
relationship between a man and a woman is the so-
called women's movement. More accurately, it may be
termed the people's movement, for as women, and
their roles in society, change, so men must adjust and
change in response. But equality, in terms of shared
responsibility between the sexes in a marriage, is not
a new concept. During the pioneer days and even up
until the 1930s, women were encouraged to grow up
rapidly and accept responsibility, to share equally in
life's struggles with the men they married. Up until
the early 1900s, a husband and wife worked side by
side. The family was an economic unit, and men and
women shared equal, if different, responsibilities. The
man was head of the household, president of the company. But the wife was executive vice-president. Both
respected the other's abilities and knowledge. They
worked as a team. In the thirties, as people left the
farms and rural areas to enter urban life, the need to
maintain the family as an economic unit diminished.
The roles shifted. The labor was divided. The man
became the breadwinner, and the woman stayed home

as the mother and housekeeper. In short, the man continued as president of the company. The woman became the custodian. With growing affluence and work-saving devices, the marriage relationship, once built on sharing the responsibilities of life, changed dramatically. Many men felt increasingly burdened by their responsibilities. Many women became more and more childlike, unable to handle the responsibilities of an adult. And many couples felt trapped. A woman who does not feel that she can work and care for herself feels trapped in a relationship. A man feels trapped by the fears of such a dependent woman.

Vaughn and Mary are caught in this snare. Mary has a college education but has not worked since she and Vaughn were married right after she finished college. She lived at home all through college and had always been taken care of, first by her parents and then by Vaughn. Within a year after their wedding, their first child was born and two years later, their second. At the tender age of forty-two, Vaughn and Mary were hit by the empty nest syndrome—hard. Both children were grown and away at college. Mary did not want to go to work but was bored staying at home. She depended on Vaughn in every way, emotionally as well as financially. She felt trapped by that dependence. Vaughn, too, felt trapped by the fear that Mary could not function if he left. Both wanted out of the snare.

Both felt trapped by Mary's complete dependence. Yet both were to blame for that very dependence: Vaughn, because he had always encouraged Mary to stay at home, not think, and rely on him for all decisions; Mary, because she so readily abdicated all responsibility. Interestingly, it was Vaughn who first began to change, who encouraged Mary to begin widening her horizons. He suggested that Mary go to work, take classes, do something to break the burden of dependency. Mary did go to work but only part-time. And her heart wasn't in it. She was unhappy with her job. In fact, that brief sojourn into the "real world" convinced her that she never wanted to work again. Mary's wish to remain a child and Vaughn's acceptance of this role have left them both feeling cheated by the other, when, in reality, they are cheating themselves by refusing to change.

During the last ten years, we have encouraged women to change their circumstances, shed their illusions, and grow up again. Many are shouldering more responsibility for themselves and becoming more active partners in their relationships—sexually, emotionally, financially. And many couples are welcoming the change. Instead of the strict division of labor, husbands and wives are sharing all sorts of responsibilities once again. As women are changing, so men are changing. And both are growing.

Robert and Claire are such a couple. They married when Robert was in college and Claire still in high school. After the wedding she worked a year while Robert finished his education. Although Claire still helps Robert in his work occasionally, she basically cares for their home and children. Yet neither feels trapped. They have a relationship of equality and respect. While they have a few close friends with whom they share their feelings, they turn primarily to each other with their emotional needs. They like their two children. They enjoy doing things with them and sharing their ups and down. But, after seventeen years of marriage, they put their relationship with each other, not the children, first.

Claire feels that she could certainly work if she wanted to, or go to college. But she does not feel a need to do this. She and Robert have so much happening in their lives that she has no interest in expanding in this way. But she doesn t feel locked in. And Robert doesn't feel burdened.

The only time either of them felt trapped was when the children had to come first, during the period between the time the first child was born and the second child entered school. Claire felt she had no time for herself. And Robert was so busy struggling to keep his own business on its feet that he was seldom home. Closeness suffered. But Robert and Claire had developed enough trust in their relationship to nurture it through this family crisis, as well as through many others.

If you ask them how they've done it, they'll laugh and tell you, "We just grew up together." The solution is not to wait until you are grown-up to establish a relationship but to recognize the need to grow and to encourage and share that growth together. In truth, we are never grown-up. Grown-up implies complete, finished, done. And that never happens. As we go through life, we are constantly changing. And that change comes in cycles. We have different needs, and thus different ideals, at different stages throughout our adult lives. One theory holds that we need to change spouses as we go through each developmental phase. The growing popularity of what has been referred to as "serial monogamy," in which individuals marry and divorce repeatedly throughout their lifetime, indicates that many people are taking this theory to heart. Perhaps this is one approach. But I do not think that it is a necessary one, or the only one. If our partner continues to grow, and so do we, we will continue to spark each other's growth. I have seen this in good marriages as well as in those in deep trouble.

Sometimes we spend years not rocking the boat, like Bill and Margaret. Their relationship appeared stable for eighteen years. Bill appeared to be very mature. An accountant with three children, he was very responsible both financially and as a father. But as a husband, he remained an adolescent. Margaret, on the other hand, was very much an adult, capable of a truly intimate relationship. After eighteen years she would no longer settle for the sterile relationship with Bill. So she insisted that they look at their marriage squarely, that they quit pretending. The list of indictments, supported by facts, against Bill was long. His affair was the crowning blow. Margaret was angry and justifiably demanding. Bill had to choose between growing up and losing his wife and family. He chose to grow up.

The major part of that growing up for Bill was untangling the apron strings that still tied him to his mother. At age forty he was still his mother's son first, his wife's husband second. Bill had never left home, really. He was still his mother's little boy—her favorite, the one who could do no wrong. As he began to wean himself from this cherished position, his mother, at age seventy, clung to him as she would a five-year-old leaving for kindergarten. Bill's greatest battle, however, was not with his mother but with himself. He had incorporated his mother's perceptions of him as a little boy within himself. They were part of him and his perceptions of himself.

These ingrained perceptions are hard to get rid of. But they must be disassembled and examined so that we can discard those parts that hamper growth. Once Bill recognized this, his change was rapid. In eight short months he learned to reach out as an adult to his wife. He learned to feel close, to talk about his feelings. The rewards were great. Bill and Margaret have discovered that being parents requires only one-tenth of their time, while it used to demand nine-tenths. And that leaves plenty of time for being together. They fight, but Bill is no longer afraid that Margaret will leave him. They make love, but Margaret is no longer just doing her duty. Instead of changing spouses, they have changed. They have done it because one partner, in this case Margaret, was committed to living, not just existing. She demanded change. In response to her demands, Bill was forced to change too. At first he was committed only to keeping Margaret. Now, like Margaret, he is committed to developing their relationship to its fullest.

WHAT IT TAKES

And that commitment takes courage. It takes honesty and work and change. It takes all these weapons to combat the seemingly innocent processes that can ruin a perfectly good marriage.

It takes courage to quit protecting, to risk, to go for broke in any relationship. It means refusing to settle for second best. It means taking a stand. It means taking your losses as well as your winnings.

It takes honesty to overcome pretense—to be open with yourself, with your partner. It means looking at your relationship and seeing what *is*, not what you would *like* to see. It means looking honestly at what you want, who you want it from, and what price (if necessary) you are willing to pay. It means conveying those desires, those feelings, openly and honestly to your partner.

And that takes work. It takes learning and practicing the skills—sharing, caring, loving—necessary to be involved with your spouse. You must be involved not just when you feel like it, not just when it's convenient, not just when you need something from your partner, but each and every day.

That work, by its definition, will spark change. And the cycle will repeat itself, for *change* is risky, threatening. It takes *courage* to let it happen, to avoid protecting the relationship all over again. It requires *honesty* to decide what that change means to you, how you feel about it, where you want the relationship to go from that point. It takes *work* to get from where you are to where you want to go, to turn what you have into what you want. And that movement, that growth, that evolution is, once again, *change*.

So, in coming full circle, we discover that we are dealing *not* with a myriad of discrete problems—protecting, pretending, loafing, resisting change. Nor are we talking about how to cope with each—applying a touch of courage here, a dash of honesty there, a pinch of elbow grease when absolutely necessary. We're dealing with a process, a cycle, a continuum, that not only fosters but helps perpetuate the intimacy and love between two people. It is a positive spiral that encourages sharing, deepens caring, generates intimacy, reaffirms commitment, and perpetuates love.

If this process has come to a grinding halt, it can be started again. If it is interrupted, it can be reset in motion. Just as in math or science, such dynamic, creative processes are usually based on simple methods. So, in relationships, I have found a simple, constructive method that can thwart our natural tendencies to protect, pretend, loaf, and resist change. I have found, in short, how not to ruin a perfectly good marriage.

5

Quitting Cold Turkey

The not-so-funny thing about nasty little habits—like protecting, pretending, loafing, and resisting change—is that they become nasty *big* habits. They have an insidious way of sneaking up on you. Delicate subjects that you let slip by "just this once" never seem to get brought up. Once under the carpet, unpleasant truths rarely find their way back out. Work put off until tomorrow somehow never quite gets done. Inertia gets a toehold, and before you realize what has happened, you're hooked on the security you *think* these habits provide.

They are tough, tough habits to break. They require that you first look squarely not at your spouse or your marriage but at yourself. Enough of this "We'd be just fine if only she would . . ." or, "If he would just change the way he . . ." Marriage makes it all too easy to lay blame for our problems, and those of the relationship, on someone else. After all, a spouse is so handy! But, unfortunately, you cannot change your partner. Not really. You can only change yourself and your response to him or her. You can only control yourself. So you are the only person for whom you can be responsible. *You* are responsible for the fact that you are in this relationship in the first place. And you are responsible, to a large extent, for what you have and what you don't, what you're getting and what you're not, what you've gained and what you've lost.

You are all you've got to start with: what you think, how you feel, what you want. And that wanting—big things, little things; some things, everything—is ultimately the ingredient that provides the courage to stop all this protecting and pretending and loafing. It provides the courage to quit, cold turkey, now.

SPEAKING UP

But wanting must be coupled with a willingness to work for what you want. And that work begins with open, honest, *daily* communication. So start talking. If something is important to you, acknowledge it. If something is bothering you, say so. If your partner has hurt you, admit it. If your feelings change, don't deny them. Talk about how you feel, what you think, what you want.

It's easy enough to say but very difficult if you have never tried. So, as with any new exercise, you should begin gradually. That means starting with just a few minutes each day, ten to begin with, talking with your partner. During that time say everything that comes to your head. Don't think of how it sounds. Just say it. And your partner will do the same.

Don't even try, during the first week or so, to listen to each other. The speaking must come first. Each partner takes five minutes to do this. If your spouse is reluctant, or even refuses, that makes it more difficult but not impossible. I have helped many couples in this way with only one person cooperating at first. The learning process takes longer, but it eventually does "take."

As you practice this spontaneous openness, it becomes habit-forming, for it increases the intensity and, hence, the intimacy and pleasure in the relationship. The important thing to remember is to focus on *feelings*, not on a minute description of what prompted them or what you think about them.

For example: "I was thinking about our relationship today and realized that we never kiss each other except to say hello and good-by. I really would like more affection than this. I know I haven't been giving more than this myself, but I recognize that I need more physical closeness—not just perfunctory or sexually-oriented affection but real closeness. I would like to change this. I don't know how it started and that isn't important.

"I just want to change this now. I feel cold and unloving without the physical affection. I have noticed that you give the children a lot of love pats and holding. Even the dog asks for, and gets, more physical affection than we give each other. Have you noticed? Does it bother you? How do you feel about it?"

If you read that aloud, you'll find that it takes less than one minute. So you can see how you can cover a lot of feelings in five minutes. This is the first step in tearing down the defenses, in increasing the intimacy in the relationship. Notice the focus is on the open, honest expression of your feelings and *not* on laying blame for those feelings. Don't begin by asking hostilely, "Why don't you ever kiss me anymore?"

If, however, your partner does not respond, you may follow up with something like this: "I've noticed since we last talked about being closer physically that I don't feel you have been very interested in trying to hold hands or kiss. This has upset me, and I guess I withdrew and did not try either. I really wanted you to be the one to reach out, and I didn't try to do it myself. Is there some reason why you don't have this need for physical closeness? Have I not given it enough time? I also recognize that if I want this type of closeness, I must do the reaching out and not wait for you to take the initiative. Let's try again. And I will try harder. I know it sounds foolish, but sometimes I am jealous of your ability to pat the children on the head and spontaneously kiss them. The flow of love seems so natural. I want it for me."

Again, no blaming—just explaining your feelings. This gives the other person a chance to talk about his or her feelings, too, without the feeling that he or she has been attacked. Oh, attack is much easier: "What's wrong with you? I need affection and I told you so last week. But you haven't done anything about it. We'll never get anywhere. You never try." But all you'll get from this approach is denial, anger, and often a stubborn refusal to try at all.

One woman to whom I was teaching this method remarked, "I have done this all my life, and my husband calls it nagging." In probing a bit further, I discovered that she was doing two things wrong. First, she was approaching her husband with, "Why don't you ever kiss me?" Second, she was resurrecting every instance in the last ten years that he neglected her in some way: "Before we were married, you always loved kissing me, and then you stopped. You just aren't romantic anymore. Why don't you kiss me or hold my hand?" Her husband was smart enough to see this as nagging, not as a sharing of feelings.

Many people will also excuse themselves by saying to me, "But you don't understand. He [she] doesn't hear me unless I yell. You have to hit a mule over the head to get his [her] attention." This may be true. So I say to get the attention any way you can. But after that, don't blame. Talk about feelings, all kinds of feelings:

angry or amorous, bitter or sweet. But again, use the "I feel," not the "you do." Don't attack with "you make me so angry!" Begin instead with "I am so angry." Then go on to explain, "I feel as though you do not hear any of my complaints or seem to care. This really hurts me, and then I become angry. I wish I could find a way to feel at least heard by you, rather than dismissed without ceremony."

This kind of expression of feelings is important. It gets your feelings out in the open without crushing the other person. It frees your partner to listen and respond rather than defend his or her actions. And it provides an opportunity to discuss the feelings on both sides.

TUNING IN

Speaking up is wasted effort unless someone is tuning in. And half the time, in a loving relationship, that someone should be you. Tuning in means seeing the other side—not as you would like to see it but as your partner does. That means listening.

Listening, really listening, requires that we throw out all preconceived ideas. Admit that you do not know your partner and that he or she does not know you. Quit believing that you can tell if he is upset by the way he walks in the door or that you know what kind of mood she is in by the way she walks. You can't and you don't no matter how long you've been together. We are constantly changing in large and small ways, so the notion "I know you" is impossible. Instead, think, "I do not know how he [or she] feels right now. I do not know what he [or she] is thinking." Then start listening. Listen when spouses tell who they are, when they tell what they want, when they tell how they feel. And that, strange as it may sound, takes courage—courage to be willing to really find out, really *want* to know, how your partner feels and courage to ask questions when you're not sure. It is far more comfortable, more secure, to be in charge and to sit back and decide how our partner feels for ourselves.

Gloria did a lot of sitting back. She had never really been interested in Arch's feelings as long as he was meeting her needs. That part she had down pat. "I feel" and "I need" punctuated almost every conversation with Arch. The only problem was that Arch felt like a father instead of a partner.

Listening did not come easily to Gloria, as it doesn't to anyone who is out of practice. It is not easy or natural or spontaneous, or always pleasant. It was, at first, very self-conscious and deliberate. It began with a cool, calculated decision. Gloria knew what she wanted, to be closer to Arch. And she knew that the only way to do that was to listen to his needs as well as to her own. At first she simply decided, "I'll be interested in whatever he tells me and ask a lot of questions." Sounds simple. But that didn't quite work. Arch, unfortunately, was not used to being listened to, so he remained quiet and withdrawn, scarcely saying a word. Finally, Gloria shouldered the responsibility, which was indeed hers, and began saying, "I want to know how you felt about what I just said. I want to know how you feel about me." Arch was dumbfounded. He couldn't believe his ears. His consternation made Gloria realize just how uncaring she had been, how blind she had become to feelings other than her own. And she began a sincere, honest effort to understand and respond to his needs.

Listening, I think, seems simpler than talking because it's so easy to fake. But phony listeners are easily spotted. Take Karl. He prided himself on his ability to communicate about problems, to really express himself, and to discuss with his wife, Marianne, both his and her feelings. But they weren't really close.

And Karl blamed Marianne, saying that she would not share her feelings. So Marianne began working on the first step, telling Karl how she felt and what she needed. She would begin, "I really would like to do something with you today," to which Karl would respond, "Fine, fine," as he gazed absent-mindedly into space. "Would you like to do something together?" Marianne would persist. "Oh, sure! I'd like to have some friends over tonight for dinner and . . ." I, I, I, I, I. Karl was so concerned with his own needs and desires that he never stopped to find out what Marianne had in mind, what *she* wanted, when she expressed her desire to share something with him that day. Those "conversations" would leave Marianne bewildered and disappointed, thinking, "What's the use? He never wants to listen." So Karl, like Gloria in the preceding example, began slowly and delibererately learning how to listen.

Listening means looking at your partner, of thirty days or thirty years, and asking, "How have you been today? What has happened to you?" Each day we, as individuals, experience new things, new feelings, new ideas. And each day, if we're lucky or determined, we change—sometimes just a fraction, sometimes dramatically. But if we do not share those changes, if we do not speak of them and have our partner receive them through listening, he or she cannot truly know or understand us. We begin to lose the sharing. Then we lose the caring. Then the intimacy goes. Then the commitment. One day we find ourselves looking across the breakfast table or the bed at a total stranger whom the minutes, then the days, then the years changed beyond all recognition. This because we did not talk. This because we did not listen.

Michael and Stephanie awoke to this shocking realization when, after nine years of marriage and one child, they discovered that they literally had nothing to talk about, nothing in common. They had married during their last year in college and, until a year ago, had both felt that they had a good marriage. It was a year ago that Stephanie decided to interrupt her career and stay at home with their baby. That decision made a drastic change in their lives together. Before that time Michael and Stephanie had both worked very hard at their careers, and smatterings of weekends were all they had to share. Now, for the first time since their honeymoon, they found themselves with plenty of time to share together but with nothing personal, nothing intimate, nothing vital to share.

As I began working with Stephanie and Michael, I found that they had plenty of the personal to talk about—pent-up feelings, harbored resentments, you name it. But there was nothing they wanted to share! Michael thought that Stephanie was a very intelligent, competent person and an excellent mother. But he resented her because he felt that she never really listened to him. She never said, "That's great!" or, "Oh, I'm so sorry that hurt you," in response to anything he said. Instead, she was always telling him what he *should* have done in such-and-such a situation. The "if you think *you* had a bad day" routine was one of her favorites. Understandably, Michael never felt that Stephanie was interested in him. So he turned to his friends and shared his feelings with them instead.

Stephanie, on the other hand, had her own set of disappointments. She felt that she was not seen at all. Not only did Michael never criticize her but he never told her anything: not that she was pretty, not that he was proud of her, not even that dinner was good. She felt that she did not exist for him. They both felt unloved, uncared for, and lonely. While they both loved each other, they could find no common meeting ground on which to express that love. Both knew what they wanted. But neither was willing to talk about it because both felt that they would not be heard or cared about.

Clearly, it was going to take more than polite conversation for Michael and Stephanie to get these feelings out in the open. It was going to take some serious graffling.

GRAFFLING

Don't bother reaching for the dictionary because this is my word, not Webster's. It's the word that I think best describes those confrontations that are often necessary in any relationship if we are to talk and *be heard*, to listen and *hear*.

Before we even open our mouths to begin, we must *grapple* with our own *fears*—fears of misunderstanding, hurting, losing. We must *grapple* with our *feelings* —our loneliness, our longing, our need to love and be loved in return. We must *graffle* with ourselves before we can graffle with our partner.

We must have the courage to look at our own feelings, to communicate them openly and honestly in spite of our fears, to demand that they be heard and acknowledged by our partner. And that's where the real graffling begins! Graffling is healthy, constructive fighting between two people. It is the interchange that gets feelings and fears out in the open, spoken and heard.

It's hard work. And it's done on your feet, standing toe to toe with your partner. It is standing up and saying what you mean. It is standing your ground, sticking to your feelings, and then standing in your partner's shoes, considering his or her feelings as well as your own. Graffling means standing—talking, shouting, screaming, if need be!—as long as it takes for each person to feel heard and understood and valued. And that may be days or hours or only minutes.

Michael and Stephanie's first real graffle lasted several weeks! And with nine years of resentment and silence built up, the weeks were not very pleasant ones. There was much accusing and getting it off the chest. Finally, amidst all the yelling, it was Michael who first summoned the courage to lower his voice and speak honestly of the real hurts, the real needs. "Just give me one thing, Steph," he said. "Listen to me. Please. I want to share what happened to me today and how I felt about it. I don't want any advice or solutions. I just want you to listen and care about what I say and how I feel." Stephanie understood and said, "I'll try to meet your needs. I'll try to really listen."

It was Stephanie's willingness to try to share Michael's problems, not solve them, that was the beginning of the opening up of their relationship. Michael's resentment began to slip away, and he became interested in trying to meet more of Stephanie's needs. Physical affection is a prime example. Stephanie loved to touch and be touched. Michael had always dodged by saying, "I'm just not the affectionate type." Now he said, "I'm not really the affectionate type, but I'm willing to learn how to show my feelings in that way." This willingness to try to meet Stephanie's needs encouraged her to be more loving toward Michael. In the past they had said simply, "I want," but never, "I am willing to give."

So often we think we know how to love because we know so well how we want to be loved. So we give our loved ones what *we*, not they, need in the way of loving. Stephanie felt loved when Michael held her. Michael, in contrast, needed verbal affirmation rather than physical affection. They were both giving the other what they themselves wanted. As they began to listen to each other, they discovered what each needed. And they began to give to one another, to express their love for each other, in a way that each could experience it.

REACHING OUT

Most people think that this is where the hard part, the work, begins—that this is where you decide what you're going to "do." Not true. If you and your spouse really tell each other how you feel, and if you both really listen to one another, you will have your answer.

Through talking, we discover what we want. Through listening, we discover what our partner wants —today, and for today only, for our needs and desires change constantly.

"I want to hold you," you say.

"I don't want to be held. I'm still mad at you about the incident last night," your partner responds.

So you've arrived at the problem. If you both really want to know and understand the other's needs as well as your own, you'll keep talking and you'll keep listening until the feelings change. You then both get what you want. Your partner gets over his or her anger after being heard and then wants to be close to you. And you get your wish because you feel close.

Unfortunately, people often try to short-circuit this process by moving directly from the statement of the problem to the solution, with no arithmetic, no working, in between. We've all had conversations with these enterprising individuals. Sometimes they are our friends, sometimes our bosses, sometimes our lovers, sometimes the taxi driver. When we confide that we are feeling very badly, for whatever reason, they rush to our aid, saying, "Have you thought of doing . . . ? You know, what you *could* do is . . . If *I* were in your shoes, I'd . . ." They offer solution after solution when all you really wanted was not *answers* but understanding, empathy, caring. You wanted someone to listen, to hear what you had to say—someone to care that you were feeling badly. You wanted someone to say, "Boy, that's terrible. I know what you mean. Let's sit on the patio and talk this thing out."

It is the talking and the listening, the *process* of sharing and caring about each other's feelings, that leads to a solution. There are no pat answers to any of the million or more problems that can arise between two people. There are only methods by which you can find your own answers. These methods—the honest acknowledgment of your feelings about what you have and what you want, the honest communication of these feelings to your partner daily, the concerned listening to your partner's side of things, and the willingness to try to meet those needs—sound simple. But it is not easy to change—to break and reform—life patterns. Yet these patterns must change if a relationship is to keep pace with the changes that are inevitable in each of us as individuals, as half of a couple. This breaking and reforming, breaking and reforming is a necessary part of the interaction—the relating—between two people in a marriage. It is at each breaking, or crisis, point in the development of a relationship that our craving for our old habits—protecting, pretending, loafing, resisting change—is the strongest, and the most dangerous.

We clutch tighter, hide more, risk less. We try to postpone the change that is inevitable during these periods, both within ourselves and in our relationships. It is precisely during these periods when courage, honesty, and work are most crucial that they are the most difficult—for everyone.

These are the painful, awkward periods of growth. And they come with predictable, if not comforting, regularity in all marriages. Recognizing these crises as periods of *normal* transition in the development of a relationship is the first step toward overcoming the fear and insecurity that drive us back to our old habits and put us well on the road to ruining a perfectly good marriage.

6

When the Going
Gets Tough

Marriage is not a destination. It is a journeying, a becoming, for two people who have chosen one another as traveling companions—hopefully for the rest of their lives. It is an extraordinary journey, both common and unique. Each couple chooses its own path, sets its own pace, carries its own past. Each couple experiences uniquely the common seasons, the cyclings, that this journey brings. These are seasons of great struggle and life; seasons of apparent rest and hibernation; seasons of disappointment and buried dreams; seasons of discovery, new insights, and joy. And each couple must face—alone—the crises, the crossroads, that are an inevitable part of this journey.

But others have traveled these roads before, have weathered the same seasons, have reached the same crossroads. In observing hundreds of couples, I have discerned five distinct crisis periods in this journeying we call marriage. Each and every one of these points marks a time of great stress and change. Each marks a time when old patterns of relating are threatened or shattered and when new patterns must be *created*, shaped and formed by the couple in response to their own changing needs, their changing perceptions, the changing "truth."

I have tested my theories on thousands of people and received thousands of nods, and smiles, of agreement and understanding in response. No matter what period people may find themselves in at the moment, they know what I'm talking about. They've been there. There is a commonality, an understanding, a sharing of a quite human path.

They recognize their own footsteps. And they know that others—just as awkward, just as gangly, just as determined, just as barefoot—follow.

THE HONEYMOON IS OVER

And we're off far sooner than we ever expect! "What happened," we wonder in disbelief as we try to adjust to simply living together, "to that idyllic first year we were promised? Where is the bliss we're entitled to? Let's get on with the happily ever after!"

It's a rude awakening to discover that, contrary to everything we ever heard or expected, the honeymoon is *over* the day we get married. And that goes for couples who have known each other three weeks or who have lived together three years, for young couples marrying just out of high school or middle-aged couples embarking on their second marriage. Almost without exception we see that day as a culmination of our relationship, not a beginning. Few of us ever realize that the real work of learning to care and be loving in our marriage is just starting.

It is this "beginning," this radical change in our lives, in our relationship with our beloved, that makes this event so critical. On this day we make one of the biggest commitments of our lives—one of complete caring and loving of another human being. It is a very "adult," mature commitment. We are trying to be completely grown-up in one day. And if we don't exactly *feel* grown-up, well then, we just make believe that we are. Formal weddings, with all their elaborate production details, are particularly conducive to this sort of charade. They place an inordinate amount of pressure to "playact," to pretend, on a young couple beginning a whole new way of life. And that pressure to carry off every production detail to the letter, to play those grown-up roles to the hilt, often carries over into the honeymoon or further, if we're not careful!

Sharon had been preparing during the entire year of her engagement to Ken for the wedding and honeymoon she envisioned as the high point of their relationship. After the whirlwind of parties and the wedding, Sharon and Ken set off for a little New England fishing village and a week of being, at last, alone together. Sharon was all set. She had read all the marriage manuals and how-to books. She had packed all the tantalizing gowns and expensive perfumes. She had collected recipes for romantic breakfasts in bed. And she (who scarcely functioned before 10:00 A.M.) was determined to rise an hour before Ken each morning so that she could bathe, dress, and be all sweet-smelling when he awoke. After all, the books counseled, she must be certain that her new husband saw her only in her best light.

But the adventure she related to me when she returned from her honeymoon was quite different from the storybook version she had envisioned. As it turned out, it was Ken (eager to fish in the early dawn) who arose early, showered, and prepared breakfast for a very sleep-tousled Sharon. To this day, thirty years later, Ken rises early, while Sharon sleeps until he calls her, not very well dressed but very well loved, to breakfast.

In many ways the honeymoon may set the tone for

a marriage. Sometimes, as for Sharon and Ken, it is one of harmony. Sometimes it is one of silent discord.

Doris and Wayne had waited until their mid twenties to marry. For three years every moment together had been intense. Their wedding was the storybook variety, with a cast of hundreds present. They were exhausted, anxious, apprehensive. Like many couples, they scarcely knew what they said or how they felt that day. The pressure of carrying off this elaborate production literally separated them from the experience. "Never mind," they told themselves. "If we can just make it through this day, the hard part will be over. The honeymoon will be terrific." So with this advance billing, they headed for the resort they had carefully chosen to relax, unwind, and get reacquainted.

Wayne wanted nothing more than to make love, sleep, and read. Doris, however, wanted to *do* things—to swim, talk, play on the beach. But when she told Wayne what she wanted, he stubbornly refused, insisting that they came there to rest. So Wayne spent the honeymoon quite content, while Doris was lonely and miserable. But they never spoke of this. Doris, in fact, never brought it up until twenty-four years and six children later, when she came to see me. When I asked about her relationship with Wayne, she told me about their honeymoon. Their relationship had not changed since that day. Doris was now a bitter, unhappy woman who wanted more and could not ask for it. And Wayne was a content, solitary man who could not understand his wife's unhappiness. Their marriage was a lonely place, devoid of sharing, caring, or closeness of any kind.

Doris and Wayne found out early how naturally protecting comes. Once we are married, there's more at stake. So we avoid rocking the boat. We bury unpleasant truths. As sexual ardor tapers off, we call it mellowing and studiously avoid the subject. We substitute compromise for sharing and find ourselves watching a lot of TV together.

The adjustment during the honeymoon period and through the first year together is a critical one in which patterns of communicating and listening and working and loving or of protecting, pretending, loafing, and resisting change are established. And once entrenched, either of these patterns—one growth-oriented, the other suicidal for the relationship—will tend to perpetuate itself.

Fighting the destructive tendencies to coddle and protect our brand-new marriage is not easy. It is far more comfortable, we find, to slip into those wife and husband roles we learned so well at our parents' knees —well enough, in fact, that on our wedding day many of us find ourselves shedding the very individuality that attracted us to one another in the first place. And society encourages us. We notice, with a growing uneasiness, a subtle and disturbing change in the way our friends react to us—even our close ones. Invitations rarely come to us as individuals, and our social life dwindles to "couples only" affairs. Friends don't call quite as often, thinking they might be interrupting something. Christmas cards begin coming to Mr. and Mrs. instead of to Ann and Bob, Keith and Marianne, or whoever we happened to be before we were married.

But there is consolation, at least, in solidarity. Visions of a lonely, solitary old age begin to fade. We relax a bit. We quit devoting so much time and energy to the relationship. After all, we're supposedly in this thing till death do us part. So we might as well take life a little easier. So the working stops. And so does the changing. And so does the relating.

It reminds me of the way I bought my first car. After months of diligent searching, I found the car of my dreams. The monthly payments would be steep, but I earned just enough to make them. So I bought the car, convinced somehow that it would run forever, automatically, effortlessly. It was not until later, and not very much later, that I learned about gas and oil and insurance and new tires. I was quite unprepared for all the work and investment required to keep that car going. It was far more than I could afford, and I had to work long hours to pay for it.

Protecting, pretending, loafing. All are tied to that beautiful illusion that love is easy, that with marriage come "happily ever after" endings. The first year of marriage is an important time of coming to grips with that illusion, of establishing patterns of honesty and ways of working together, of learning to mesh two often very different ways of living.

How do we learn to do this? Where do we learn about marriage? Where are the schools? Where are the apprenticeships? Actually, we all had them. And they lasted eighteen years or thereabouts. For the first place we learned about marriage was in our home, where we observed how our parents worked out the problems in their marriage. In most instances our parents serve as our model for marriage, either one to pattern ourselves after or one to rebel against. If our parents had a good marriage, by the time we reach the altar, we will have learned a lot of skills by just living with a happy couple. But suppose our parents had an unhappy life together or a very unhealthy marriage? Then we go into marriage with a severe handicap.

This donning of inherited roles, positive or negative, is one of the primary ways in which cultural patterns are passed on from generation to generation. This occurs in all cultures and is essential for the learning, the progression, and the continuation of a way of life. In a primitive society this type of learning creates no problems because individuals are taught alike in their very small, closely knit groups. There are few conflicts in values. In our very complex society—with its many levels, shifting values, and rapid change—these inherited roles may become obsolete almost before we know it.

And, too often, we fail to recognize this. By the time we are adults, we often overlook the fact that we have a choice in the matter, an opportunity to examine what has been taught to us and to decide what is valuable and what is a hindrance to us in developing and living our own lives. If we do not examine our inheritance in this way, we are apt to adopt antiquated living patterns that restrict our own development. When we impose a role upon ourselves, we do not allow our own uniqueness to develop. Certainly, we all learn by observing others and trying on their ways of relating to life. This only becomes a problem when we do it without thinking and therefore relinquish our ability to choose whether to keep or give up this type of behavior. And far too many couples do just that.

I have seen many couples after years of marriage and asked them about their parents' relationship. Over 80 percent described a relationship similar to their own, without any conscious awareness of the similarities. So these people inherited, rehearsed scripts for, a relationship that may or may not have had anything to do with their own.

I once counseled two generations of a family who clearly illustrated how strong, and how damaging, this legacy can be. I had worked with the parents for several months before the son and daughter-in-law came to see me. The father, an accountant, was the strong, silent type who felt that telling your wife about your job or yourself or your feelings was absolutely unthinkable. His life was neatly divided into manageable compartments: work and clients, wife and family. He loved his wife but saw her as someone to take care of, not share with. It was not until they were age sixty that they decided to try to change this pattern. Meanwhile the son had patterned himself after his father—holding his wife at arm's length, taking good care of her. When he was thirty, his wife told him, "I don't want to end up a lonely old woman like your mother. Either you change or I'm getting out." The son then had to take a hard look at the kind of life he wanted. He decided that he wanted to share with his wife, to care *for* her rather than take care *of* her. Until the son looked at his way of relating, he could not change. It is not necessarily that our parents' way of relating is not all right for them. It is that it cannot be simply superimposed onto a new relationship without hurting that relationship by limiting the opportunity for new expression.

It is critical, during the first year of marriage, for a couple to find their own way of relating to each other, not as their parents had done or had not done but their own unique way. This is tough to do. It requires that a couple treat each new aspect of their relationship as just that—new, unique to them. Then they must share it in a unique way. It's a lot more work than most people are willing to go to.

Greg and Julie found it almost impossible during their first year together. Greg had come from a very traditional family in which he had learned that the role of the husband was to earn the living, come home after work, and be taken care of by the wife. And Julie was more than willing to take care of him! The daughter of a mother who turned over the nurturing of her family to maids and governesses, Julie was bound and determined to be everything that her mother was not. "If I care for Greg in a different way," she told herself, "our marriage will be good, will be loving, will be safe."

So, that first year, she tried to work full time, keep

an immaculate house, cook a five-course meal each night, and be sexually inviting twenty-four hours a day. Despite the fact that she was frequently ill, Julie continued to expect the impossible of herself. Finally, toward the end of their first year together, she had had it. She exploded at Greg. He was selfish, she said. She was tired, she said. She wanted to share life, not be Greg's servant.

Julie had spent the entire first year of their marriage trying to be a "good wife." And at the end of that year, instead of feeling blissfully married, she felt used and bitter. In her anger she quit pretending and demanded change. Slowly and tediously, Greg and Julie began to discard the roles they had inherited. They began to treat their marriage as unique and learned how to develop the kind of relationship that worked for *them*, not their parents. They began to share responsibility on an equal basis, being receptive to each other's needs and together finding solutions that worked for them.

Getting on an even keel as a couple during this first year or so of marriage is essential to set up the positive habits of sharing, caring, and working necessary to weather the next impending crisis: the family.

AND BABY MAKES THREE

It's tough enough for two people to learn to relate to one another in a marriage. But it's even tougher when a third party, a baby, is thrown into the mix because now there is another person who requires relating to. As if the wife and the husband scripts weren't hard enough to get rid of, we now add father and mother roles and all their attendant expectations: "Of course you'll feel like parents immediately! Why *certainly* you'll love that little bundle of joy right away!"

Most certainly *not!* Learning to love a baby is like learning to love any other person. From the day it is born, if not before, you feel a sense of responsibility for the baby because of its dependence on you. But you cannot love this particular baby until you get to know it. Each baby is a unique individual from birth. It takes time to learn how to relate to its particular "personality." And that takes hard work, like learning to be loving toward anyone.

It's analogous to the distinction between being *in love* and *loving*. When two people are expecting their first child, they are in love with the idea of the baby. When the baby is born, they have to learn to love this unique individual. That's where the work comes in. It's work to learn how to be loving toward a baby, as it is toward any human being. The fantasy of having a baby is easy.

The crisis that a couple faces when their first child is born stems, again, from the conflict between what they expect versus what they find, magic and make-believe associated with the perfect family versus the reality of 2:00 A.M. feedings and the total dependency of another human being whom, at first (God forbid that you should admit it!), you do not love.

We often harbor fantasies of the perfect family (which *none* of us ever had but were always positive existed somewhere)—laughing, loving, living life together. Accepting this as pure fantasy is not easy. Having a baby is one of the greatest crises we, either individually or as a couple, will ever face. A child is not a play toy or a doll or a pet we can train to do just what we want. A baby is a person, and often an extremely trying one on a relationship.

But with only one year of medical residency remaining, Nick and Ann decided that they were ready for that person. It was not an easy decision. Like most couples today, and unlike most of the past, Ann and

Nick realized full well that they had a host of options. Many of their friends were postponing their families until they were well into their thirties. Still others were choosing to remain childless. So there was much planning, with many late-night discussions. But finally they decided. And with that decision Ann abandoned the pill she had taken almost every morning for the last eight years.

Much to her disappointment, Ann wasn't pregnant within a month. So she and Nick embarked on a "sex for pregnancy" marathon with all the attendant temperature charts and mid-month luncheon rendezvous! Ann was pregnant within six more weeks. And the day that she and Nick went to see *their* obstetrician—after all, this was *their* pregnancy—was a day of great excitement. They celebrated that evening with dinner out, reveling in the wonder of having a child.

Nick wanted to tell the world immediately. But Ann insisted that they savor this secret for a few days, just the two of them. And so they did. A few days later they broke the news. Then began one of the longest, and shortest, waits of their lives. Seven months is all they had to prepare, as best they could, for a completely different world.

The first four months were easy. For Ann and Nick, as for most couples, it was a period of great excitement, anticipation, and closeness. Ann experienced no physical discomfort and kept her diminutive figure until well into the fourth month of pregnancy. Having a baby was a cinch, they thought.

But then things began to change. Suddenly, or so it seemed, Ann was different. One day toward the end of the fourth month, she exclaimed, "Oh! It just kicked!" And Nick eagerly rushed to feel the growing life tucked under the batik maternity smock, which Ann, like most first mothers, could hardly wait to get into.

That marked the beginning of what I call the cocoon phase for Ann. It is during the fourth month of pregnancy that the mother to be begins wrapping herself in a cocoon of contentment. She becomes increasingly calm and introspective, more and more involved with the baby growing inside her. She enters a world of her own, a peaceful world where her husband cannot join her. Meanwhile, back in the real world, he is left to cope as best he can with her growing distance, her waning sexual interest.

Nick, like most husbands, began to feel more than a little left out. After all, it was supposed to be *their* baby! Feeling that first kick was fun. But after the tenth time it was losing some of its charm, especially now that Ann appeared to be more interested in her rapidly growing stomach than in him. She scarcely listened when he tried to tell her of an interesting patient he had seen that day. Instead she would interrupt (for the hundredth time!) with, "Hey! Feel that? I think the baby just rolled over!"

Suffering a great sense of loss, Nick found himself resenting this change in Ann. He began to feel that she was not interested in him, that she was too self-contained to care about his needs. He needed her closeness, and when it was apparently denied him, he needed it even more. But Ann was so enveloped in motherhood that she did not even notice that Nick felt left out and lonely. Her sexual appetite was at a low ebb at this point, while his was increasing in proportion to his growing need for more intimacy in their relationship. And he interpreted her waning enthusiasm for sex, again, as a waning interest in him.

For Ann and Nick, as for most couples, this pattern lasted about three months—until the seventh month or so of pregnancy. That was when, almost as suddenly as she had lost it, Ann regained her interest in Nick! She felt bulky, unattractive, vulnerable. She had always been a very pretty young woman, aware that men usually took at least a second look at her. Suddenly she realized that no one was even taking a first look. What was wrong with her, she wondered? A long, hard look in the full-length mirror on her closet door held the answer. Her face was the same, all right. But the rest of her was almost laughable. She could forgo the flattering interest of other men. But she could not do without that interest from Nick. She needed reassurance that he still found her attractive. She needed him close. She needed to share with him, both emotionally and sexually. But Nick was afraid that they might hurt the baby. At least that was part of it. The other part was, quite frankly, that he *was* less attracted to Ann. He had "turned down" his sexual thermostat in response to her previous lack of interest.

But during the last month before the baby was due, Ann and Nick came full circle. They began to talk more, to spend more time together painting the baby's room, buying baby furniture, and practicing all the techniques they learned in their Lamaze classes. They worked together on these exercises—breathing, counting, breathing, counting—because they wanted to share the labor and the joy of the delivery. They drew close again, in the joy and fear of their shared realization that soon there would be three of them—very soon.

The night that Ann felt the first mild twinges of labor, she frantically shook Nick awake to announce resolutely, "I've changed my mind! I like it better with just the two of us," as if imploring Nick to *do* something about the impending predicament. He just laughed and said, "It's a little late to be deciding that!" as he tucked Ann and her carefully packed suitcase in the car and headed for the hospital.

Sharing in the labor and delivery was very important to both Ann and Nick. They spent the day together from start to finish, and Nick was with Ann the moment they discovered that they were the parents of a baby girl. Such sharing, thanks to Lamaze and similar programs, reduces the fear and anxiety for both the new mother and father. The father who paces impatiently in a cold waiting room is without knowledge. And the mother, alone with strangers in a sterile and unknown hospital, is without loving support.

When I visited Nick and Ann in the hospital three days later, I was not surprised to see a happy, still expectant father who could not wait to show off *his* new baby in the nursery. Nor was I surprised to see Ann with a smile dutifully pasted on for the guests, halfheartedly opening a pile of fuzzy pink presents. When I gave Ann my gift, a *very* sexy nightgown for her to wear when she felt like being Ann again, she burst into tears. "I've been so depressed today," she sobbed. "You are the first person to care for me alone. Nick and all the others are more interested in the baby than in me!"

Of course, having been through this process with other couples, I knew how much, at this moment, Ann needed personal attention and care. Yet just when the new mother most needs to be pampered and loved, the new father (her husband in a very recent former life) is becoming so involved with the baby that he scarcely notices her! She has been strangely transformed from a person and a lover into something called a mother, with a capital *M*.

At first that is *not* a comfortable feeling! She realizes that her relationship with her husband is changing—that she is supposed to act like a mother now. But she doesn't know how. She doesn't feel the way the books tell her she should feel. She feels tired, needy, irritable. And often these psychological conflicts contribute as much as the drastic physical changes to the "after baby blues."

The first six weeks are the most trying. I encourage all new parents to have as much outside help as possible to manage the daily details of living when mother and baby arrive home because new parents need their energy to learn a lot of new tasks. And the biggest task facing them is learning how to love that new person who has been thrust into their lives, that interloper who sleeps peacefully during the day and demands food and attention and caring all night. Until it happens to you, it's impossible to imagine how much work that takes. Contrary to everything we've been told, it's not like turning on a tap. The feelings of love associated with parenting, for mothers *and* fathers, do not just flow spontaneously. Holding and cuddling the baby during feeding and playing are not only essential for the baby's mental health but also for the parents and child to learn how to be close. This begins the process of loving *this* particular baby, of holding him or her close and feeling the warmth of that little body against our own. Both mothers and fathers should rock and feed their new babies as much as possible, for new parents need the effect of this physical closeness as much as the baby does.

There is so much to learn. We read all the books. And we are exhausted from the anxiety of trying to do everything just right. Yet many of us are ashamed of our feelings, fearing that they are not normal or "right." For instance, it is not uncommon for a father to feel terribly jealous, seeing the new baby as a threat to his relationship with his wife. Or, the mother may experience hostility toward the child when she discovers that it is not just a plaything for her enjoyment. Such feelings are not unusual. But they make the courage to discuss these feelings openly even more imperative.

Often both parents are so anxious that they have trouble sharing these feelings with each other. This is one of the easiest times to fall back on the old "Mom" and "Dad" roles and pretend that being parents is the most important thing in life now.

By the time Ann and Nick's daughter had passed her six-week checkup, the couple had worked through these anxious feelings and realized that being close to each other and sharing in loving the baby was what having a family was all about. They were ready to be more involved with each other. Sex was becoming important to both of them again. This took a little longer for Nick than for Ann. It was more difficult for him to see Ann as a person instead of as the mother of their child. And he found making love to a mother a bit unnerving. But as Ann began to demand that she be seen as Ann—that she be taken out to dinner and on long, quiet walks—Nick began to see her once again as a person and a lover. I like to think that my gift to her in the hospital helped! But, more truthfully, it was Ann's strong sense of herself as a person first and a mother second that helped her and Nick move quickly through this period.

For some couples, it may take as long as a full year to get through this readjustment phase and reestablish what I call couple closeness. But this is a critical step if the couple is not to lose its identity in the roles of Mother and Father, destined to eternally, hopefully, futilely live out reruns from "Father Knows Best."

With this couple closeness firmly established, the relationship and the family begin to develop stability —roots. Not until roughly ten years later are these roots ripped up again for careful scrutiny.

IS THAT ALL THERE IS?

From the time the first baby is born until our children reach school age, most of our time, attention, energy, and love is absorbed by our family. A friend of mine, a young father in his late twenties, summed it up: "It's all I can do to just keep the continuity of my life going!"

But by the time we are around thirty, generally between the eighth and thirteenth year of marriage, we discover that we have enough breathing room to reassess—to take a good, hard look at—our spouse and our marriage. Men and women going through this ten-year crisis often share the same feelings: "I married him [her] because I knew what he [she] could become. And boy, has he [she] ever disappointed me!"

It is a time of great turmoil and confusion. We are restless. We are unsure. Time becomes a limiting factor. Unquestionable decisions of the past become questionable. And "now" looks like our very last chance to change. Certainly, change is inevitable during this period—change in ourselves, change in the relationship, but not necessarily change in spouses. In helping many couples through this crisis, I am convinced that, for the most part, divorce is not the answer. I have found that people who change spouses at this point tend to remarry someone just like the person they left behind. So in ten more years they're up against the same crisis. They have just postponed the inevitable confrontation with themselves.

Certainly, divorce is one option. And, in the opinion of many, an all too easy one at that. But the growing acceptance of divorce as an alternative by couples going through this crisis has some very positive side effects. These couples want more from their marriages. They are trying to be more honest with each other. They realize that unless they work to improve their relationship, divorce is a very real possibility. This was not true even ten years ago, when divorce was too terrible an option to even consider except as a last resort. So I am saying that this growing acceptance of divorce may actually help today's marriages, those that last. For the people who stay married today, more so than ever in the past, do so by choice.

There are other alternatives or, more accurately, attempts to resolve this crisis. An affair is a popular one. It looks like a relatively simple solution to the lack of intimacy in a person's life. But simple solutions are rarely found for complex problems. And, more often than not, an affair only further complicates the matter. But affairs can be instructive, although they usually exact a painful price.

Jamie had never known what Ross was asking for when he demanded closeness until, after twelve years of marriage, she had an affair. Ross had always wanted an intimate relationship with Jamie; he wanted to feel close, talk openly, share life. He tried almost everything without success. And he blamed that failure, as often as he could get away with it, on his job of eight years, which took him out of town at least three weeks out of every four. It wasn't until his position changed, and he found himself gone only one week each month, that Ross had to face facts: He and Jamie had less of a relationship than he had believed possible. They never talked about feelings that were important. They avoided confrontation. They were lost in their make-believe world of the perfect American family: the handsome, successful husband; the attractive, refined wife; the "golden couple," seen at the right social clubs, playing tennis with the right crowd. They were trapped on the surface of what appeared to be the perfect marriage. And Jamie was quite content on that surface. She saw no need to change. She had no desire for closeness. She had no real interest in sex. What she had instead was a booming part-time interior design business, which she had developed in Ross's absence. And she had many friends. In short, she had made quite a nice life for herself. It seemed, in fact, that she was happiest when Ross was away.

Then, one month when Ross was away, she began an affair; she fell magically in love and finally realized what Ross had been talking about all those years. She learned to enjoy being close, emotionally and physically. And she recognized that this was what Ross had always known and wanted. Jamie came to me in a state of great confusion. "I am involved with another man," she said. "I know now that I have a choice—to divorce Ross and marry this man or stick with my marriage. And I don't know what I want."

In talking with Jamie, I soon discovered how little she and Ross shared. They saw each other as intimate enemies, not as best friends. There was no intimacy, no acceptance. And, perhaps most important at this point in their marriage, there was no feeling of mutual trust, not just in terms of fidelity but in terms of caring and commitment. To make matters worse, Jamie was unquestionably untrustworthy at this time. But she finally realized that this was not the man for whom to divorce Ross. He was too much like Ross. She knew something had to change. And she decided that it would be her relationship with her husband.

She knew it must begin with talking. She had found it very easy to talk with her lover, for they had so much to say in just getting to know each other. It was easy for Jamie to admit that they were strangers. It was much harder to admit that, after twelve years of marriage, she and Ross were just as much strangers. So Jamie began with the premise that before they could go anywhere, before they could even decide whether or not their marriage was worth salvaging, she and Ross needed to get acquainted.

Their initial efforts were very awkward and stilted. In the past a typical conversation had consisted of Jamie's halfhearted inquiry about Ross's day, followed by a detailed report of the children's activities. Now Jamie began asking Ross to really share his day, not just what he did but how he felt. She began to really listen to his answers, to be interested, to ask questions. And she began to talk about herself and how she felt, not just about what she did each day. From Ross's example, she learned by listening how to express her own feelings in words. At first Ross was so resentful that he could not accept the changes in Jamie. "For ten years, I've wanted you, and you would not respond," he charged. "I hate you for that loss." It took a solid year of fighting, wanting to separate, and fighting some more for Ross to work through his resentment and for Jamie to learn to show her love for him openly.

Jamie and Ross got more than acquainted. They got to know one another and themselves. And in the process—in the sharing and the caring and the deepening intimacy—their relationship became increasingly solid, increasingly secure. They quit protecting their relationship only to find that they *could* trust in one another's caring, that they could say what they felt without fear. They quit pretending that they had the perfect marriage. They got to work. And they began to change.

One important aspect of their marriage that they wanted to change, to work on, was their sexual relationship. Jamie had always perceived sex as a duty, not as an exciting or rewarding expression of love. During her brief affair she had learned a great deal about her own body and her sexual needs. She knew what she wanted and needed. And she knew that she had to ask for it openly and honestly. When she told Ross that she felt that their sexual relationship was dull and routine, he was surprised but relieved that her feelings paralleled his own. With that honest admission, they could begin to change their approach to sex. They began to spend a great deal of time discussing their own sexual needs and fantasies. They began experimenting, discovering many things they enjoyed and some they didn't. Sex now is a unique experience for Ross and Jamie. Each time it expresses something new about their relationship to each other.

What Ross and Jamie have now is not perfect, and it never will be. But that is precisely what keeps their relationship growing, moving always toward something more, something better, something closer.

Getting started isn't easy. Ross and Jamie discovered how difficult it is during this period to trust enough, to have faith enough, in both your and your partner's real ability to grow and love to refuse to settle for second best. When we have ten years or so invested in something, like a marriage, we do everything in our power to hang on to it. And the more we doubt, the more we deny the truth. The more we fear, the tighter we clutch to what we have. We pretend. We protect. And we paralyze our relationship.

George and Cindy managed to accomplish this in a record six years of marriage, thanks to the stifling methods of protecting that both employed! Cindy was terrified of life and had married George at a very young age so that she would have someone to take care of her. Only two years her senior, George was Cindy's father and mother all rolled into one. George spoiled her and found all sorts of excuses for her childish behavior. If something upset Cindy, George made sure it didn't happen again. If something frightened her, George protected her. Because Cindy behaved as a child, she could not respond to George as an adult, either sexually or emotionally.

They had no friends. Cindy did nothing without George, nothing with a girl friend, nothing alone, nothing. When they came home from work, Cindy would do all the household chores—cook dinner, wash dishes, do laundry—and then hibernate. Although he occasionally would busy himself with odd jobs around the house, George usually spent evenings parked in front of the TV, relaxing. They almost never went out. Cindy's fears governed their lives. And as those fears grew, life together became increasingly restricted.

When Cindy and George came to see me, I demanded that Cindy behave as an adult and that George support, not protect, her. Every time he said, "Oh, it's all right if Cindy doesn't do that," I insisted, "No, George, she must. And you must stand back and let her do it for herself." One thing Cindy did for herself was to find an interest to pursue on her own, apart from George. She chose softball, a team sport that she had enjoyed in high school. She joined her company's team and began to get acquainted with some of the other women in her office. At first, Cindy was so shy and withdrawn that she could scarcely say hello to her teammates. But she was determined. She signed up for every game. She shared a pizza afterward with the team. She even began to get together with some of the women on weekends. She became more self-confident. She began to grow in a world of her own, not in George's shadow.

As Cindy began succeeding at being an adult, George found that he liked her better. Their relationship was making significant strides, in George's opinion, until the crisis hit. Suddenly, or so it seemed to him, Cindy was becoming entirely too independent. As her personal security grew, George's dwindled. There was no doubt about it; he was losing control! The real crisis came when Cindy realized that she was enough of her own person to live without George—when she realized that she had a choice. And she chose to stay married to George, not because she needed to but because she wanted to.

Then the tables turned, and Cindy began to make a few demands of her own! She demanded that George begin sharing the household responsibilities so that they would both have more time to do other things. Cindy loved to cook, so George began to help each evening by setting the table and doing the dishes with Cindy after the meal. Given the options, he also decided that, of all the household chores, he minded vacuuming least, while Cindy hated it the most. A perfect match. This sharing of household responsibilities gave both Cindy and George a chance to pursue other interests, either individually or together.

And, speaking of pursuing interests together, Cindy had a few demands in that department too. She wanted to *do* things together, *be* together, not just pass the time in each other's company. She wanted a day together. She wanted Sunday. When she told George about her feelings, he went along only half-heartedly, in a very self-sacrificing way. When Cindy would suggest a day on the beach, a walk in the woods, or even just a movie, George would dutifully but grudgingly shoulder his responsibility as chauffeur and escort. But there was no real sense of sharing. Some fun. When Cindy explained that this was not quite what she had in mind, George would whine, "But I'm doing what you asked. Aren't you ever satisfied?"

Cindy's frank answer was "No. I want more. And *I am willing to give more.*" So she kept wanting and demanding and expecting and giving more. She started simply. One Sunday it was, "Let's go out for breakfast." The next Sunday it was, "Let's go out for breakfast again. But first, how about a jog in the park?" She began to come up with ideas for activities they would both enjoy doing. And, more important, she began to talk about her feelings, good and bad, just as they came into her head. This openness, this spontaneity, this honesty on Cindy's part encouraged George to respond in the same way. Soon George found that he began to look forward to Sundays as much as or more than Cindy.

It was essential that Cindy develop first as an adult before she and George could develop this kind of healthy give-and-take relationship built on mutual respect and caring. And that required that George quit protecting both Cindy and their relationship.

This protecting kept them safe, or so they thought. By keeping Cindy totally dependent, George could be relatively secure in the knowledge that she was not going to leave him. Now they realize that they have a choice. They stay together now not out of dependency but out of mutual respect and caring.

Sometimes we try to protect our partner, as George did Cindy. Sometimes we try to protect ourselves. We don't want to be hurt or rejected, so we don't take chances. We don't ask for what we want and need. We don't demand it. Sex is a particularly vulnerable issue during this ten-year crisis. It is usually during this period that a man seeks more adventure in sex but is often afraid to share his desires with his wife, particularly if he wants something quite different from their previous pattern. This inability to ask directly for what either partner wants usually finds frustrated expression in other ways.

I once counseled two young women who were both trying to understand what was happening in their respective marriages of ten years. I did not see the husbands in either case, but the symptoms in the marriages were identical, and classic. "He is irritable," each wife explained. "He seems unhappy with me. Nothing satisfies him. He's very successful, but he wants to move up the business ladder more quickly." When I inquired about the sexual aspects of their relationship, each woman told me, "We haven't tried anything different in years."

Again, I do not teach sexual technique but instead encourage people to be creative, to express their sexuality in their own way—a way that pleases them. There are just so many basic ways to make love. But the way *we* as individuals make love is uniquely our own. So I encourage each person to experiment, to discover what is pleasurable to himself or herself and to his or her partner.

The cardinal rule, which I emphasized with these two women, is "Do not protect your husband. You are to be open with your needs and requests. Do not wait to find out what he wants. Know what you want and then find out what he wants." After understanding the source of their husbands', and their own, dissatisfaction with the lack of vitality and intimacy in their marriages, both of these young women began to change. Instead of falling back on the old excuse of "if only he were different," these women recognized that you don't have to change partners to have a different relationship. You only have to change yourself. This change will then spark change in your partner. I have seen this repeatedly as I work with only one half of a couple, the wife or husband. I watch and help one partner change. And we both find that the spouse changes as well.

In fact, it is often individual growth and change during this period that precipitates change in the relationship. When the last of Craig and Patsy's three children was seven years old, Patsy suddenly felt boring and bored. After twelve quite contented years of being involved with her growing family, she was tired of the "old Patsy." At age thirty-five she found that home, family, and community—which the old Patsy had found very satisfying—just weren't enough for the "new Patsy." She was changing. She needed something more. She needed something different. She considered dusting off her teaching certificate or polishing up her typing skills. But neither of these appealed to the new Patsy. So she began looking for a job that met her needs—that put her in contact with interesting people, that rewarded her financially for her performance, and that gave her the flexibility to be with the children when they needed her. And she found one, as an advertising salesperson for a local magazine.

Anything that sounds too good to be true usually is. So, into this tale, enter the not-so-charming prince—her husband, Craig. Craig was very disturbed by this new Patsy. He was threatened and tried everything in his power to dissuade her. "Who will take care of the children?" he wanted to know. "Are you trying to tell me I don't make enough money for you? What will our parents think about your leaving the family? Aren't we enough for you?" Feelings, and tempers, ran high on both sides. This crisis forced Craig and Patsy to examine carefully what they valued in life, both individually and with respect to their relationship. When they began to talk about these wants, these needs, Craig's real fear came to the forefront: He was afraid that Patsy would quit loving him. He needed reassurance. He needed Patsy's affection and interest in him as a person. And he began to ask more directly for what he needed.

Patsy realized that she had been so dissatisfied with her own life that she had completely ignored Craig's needs. Now that she had accepted responsibility for meeting her own needs for self-fulfillment, she and Craig could concentrate on meeting each other's personal needs in the relationship. Patsy began to listen to Craig, to give what he needed to feel less threatened by the changes in her. She also began to express her own needs more directly, asking Craig to give her, in return, the very things he was asking from her.

Now these changes required some rather drastic

modifications in their life-style. And that meant some rather drastic conflicts. Craig did not assume his share of the household chores too cheerfully. And the children did not give up their chauffeur, servant, and short-order cook without a fight. But these problems seemed almost to solve themselves as Patsy and Craig concentrated on meeting each other's personal needs first and then shared in solving the other problems.

The changes were remarkable—first in Patsy, who found a new energy and vitality in her expanding role as wife, mother, and businesswoman; and then in their marriage. Craig now takes pride in his equal partnership with Patsy. He enjoys sharing responsibility with her. And she has a stronger appreciation and respect for that responsibility.

If a couple resists this kind of change during the ten-year crisis, the partners pay a terrible price in constant dissatisfaction. If they welcome it, their love can deepen to a level that brings greater satisfaction and a heightened degree of intimacy. No longer do they find that they are talking "at" each other. They feel, instead, that they are "being" together—not fused together but solidly together, by choice.

Ross describes it this way: "I used to be jealous of Jamie's involvement with tennis and the children because we had so little intimacy in our marriage. Now, with the growing sense of closeness between us, these independent activities only seem to enhance our relationship. Each of us now has something to bring to the whole. And I can enjoy Jamie's tennis activities with her by sharing her excitement." So doing everything together is the last thing that Ross and Jamie want or that their relationship needs. But this couple of fourteen years still spend five to ten hours each week talking about their feelings and their relationship.

The ten-year crossroad marks the time to become lovers again. The children are older. There is more time for individual and joint pursuits. It is a time for a wife to see her husband not just as a breadwinner, not just as a father, not just as a companion, but as a man, and her lover. It is a time for a husband to see his wife not just as a polished Wonder Mother or career woman, not just as a loving mother, not just as a confidante, but as a woman, his lover. It is a time for each partner to be seen as special and important, not to be criticized and found wanting. It is a time to give what a partner needs and to accept and love what he or she may offer in return.

This acceptance—first of ourselves, with all of our assets and limitations, and then of our spouse—is one of the common ingredients I have noted in couples who have weathered this crisis. And this acceptance is the root of the peace we establish both with and within ourselves. It is more a truce really. It is a time of love and growth—a time to establish the trust, the openness, the honesty in our marriage that we will so desperately need when that peace shatters.

THE BIKINI CRISIS

A forty-year-old man who came to see me many years ago had fallen magically in love with an airline stewardess half his age. When I asked him why, he replied, "She looks terrific in a bikini." That was my introduction to what I now call the bikini crisis—a deceptively coy euphemism for what I truly believe is one of the most critical periods in our lives, both as individuals and as a couple. It is during this particular crisis period, after roughly twenty years of marriage, that we often make our worst, and most irrevocable, mistakes.

The first three crises in the development of a relationship—marriage, the family, the ten-year syndrome —all pale by comparison. They are like the developmental phases of a child. But the bikini crisis has all the turmoil, all the torment, all the upheaval of adolescence.

It is as much physical as psychological. The signs of time passing become much more difficult to mask. Lady Clairol and toupees enjoy their finest hour. Hormonal changes as women approach menopause serve as undeniable reminders that our options are narrowing. Physiological changes in men, currently referred to as "male menopause," wreak havoc on what were once stable, orderly, and satisfactory lives. Now nothing seems satisfactory. Nothing seems to be enough. We want something more. We want something different.

It is a desperate, crazy period. And people in the throes of this crisis appear to be just that: desperate and crazy. They are trying to run away from their problems. They literally cannot perceive that the problems are within themselves. Men, and many women, at this point feel that the die is cast in terms of their career. It's too late to change jobs. So that leaves them with their marriage—their spouse. Women, if they have not chosen to pursue a career, also focus on their marriage, on their spouse, as the source of their desperate dissatisfaction. Too often men and women see the answer to their confusion, their turmoil, in changing partners rather than in changing their relationship to them. Certainly, that looks like the simplest route.

It was a route that John, ultimately, could not resist. In the twenty years John and Katherine had been married, they had realized their dreams together. John had built a business from scratch and finally "made it." They had every material luxury they had ever dreamed of. They had two attractive, intelligent, ambitious daughters, one in college and the other in high school. They had truly shared life, both the good and the bad. They liked and respected each other. They were open, honest, trusting in their relationship. They were friends. They were lovers.

Then it hit. The first hint came when John asked Katherine, an attractive woman with graying temples, to bleach her hair. Next, he instigated a shopping trip to buy her a brand-new wardrobe. He even went so far as to suggest a plastic surgeon for her face-lift. While Katherine had difficulty understanding these new demands, she did as John asked but drew the line at the face-lift. She became a new person on the outside, saying, "If John finds me more pleasing this way, that's all that matters." Of course, Katherine's "outside" had nothing to do with the problem hidden deep in John's "inside." John became impotent and blamed her for not being sensuous enough. One day he walked in after work and announced that he loved another woman, that he wanted to be free. John was so desperate by this point that he actually considered staging a fake accident and having himself declared legally dead to rid himself of his present life.

Despite Katherine's efforts to help him, to change with him, they separated and divorced. John married and divorced three times—each time to a very young and attractive woman. He neglected his business. He squandered most of his assets. Unable to face the ruin he was bringing upon himself, he began running physically, to exotic places in foreign lands.

Katherine waited through two of these marriages, hoping that John would someday return to their relationship. When she finally accepted that that would never happen, she met and married a very supporting, stable man. But even now, ten years later, she has not stopped loving and caring for John. John is now married for the fourth time, this time to a woman only ten years younger than him. She has four children. She is very much like Katherine. And John has begun rebuilding his life with her. The tragedy, of course, is that John is only now beginning to work on the problems he might have resolved ten years ago with Katherine if he had only realized what was happening to him, inside him. But he could not see his behavior as irrational. He wanted to be free. He wanted to love in a magical way.

Marty and Janice handled this crisis quite differently. They, like John and Katherine, had lived a charmed life for more than twenty years together. With four children ranging in age from six to twenty, they were the perfect couple—the perfect parents, the perfect community leaders, the perfect friends. Only one thing was missing: They were not the perfect lovers. They had no intimacy, no intensity in their relationship. They never talked to each other about their feelings. They were never able to be honest and open with one another. Their sex life was dull and listless.

While Marty had always been very much opposed to extramarital affairs, he had strayed more than once in a casual way during the past two years. He was unhappy with his job. He was unhappy with Janice. He felt uncreative. He felt dead. And he thought another woman might fix all that. So, like John, he fell magically in love with a younger woman. When he came to see me, he was feeling miserable about feeling miserable. But he wanted to leave Janice and at least give his newfound relationship a try.

The difference between Marty and John was that Marty was not afraid to look at *himself*, as well as his relationship with Janice. He was able to see that he was behaving, reacting, like an adolescent. He loved Janice as a sister and did not want to hurt her. But all was magic with the other woman. He was in love. He could talk about his feelings and share his doubts, his fears, his dreams. Sex with her was free and uninhibited. And he would not give that up. What he agreed to do instead was work on his relationship with Janice to see if his feelings about her, and hence the other woman, might change. Janice did her part. Although she never knew about the affair, she knew what was at stake. It was not easy. For instance, Janice had never been particularly fond of sex. She had never known what it was all about really. So she had always been very withdrawn and inhibited. When Marty explained that he needed more involvement, more participation, more sharing, more intimacy in their sexual relationship, Janice got to work. She enrolled in a course on sexuality at the local junior college—not to learn anything new, particularly, but to desensitize herself. I also worked with her to help her accept her own sexuality. Much to her and Marty's delight, sex became a great adventure. As their sexual relationship took on more depth and intensity, so did their emotional relationship. They began to learn to be more open with one another, to share fears and dreams.

As his relationship with Janice changed, Marty was able to say good-by to his mistress. He and Janice both acknowledge that their relationship is not perfect, as they and everyone else once thought. But there is no such thing as a perfect relationship. What they do have, and work hard to maintain, is a relationship of closeness and openness that gives their lives together vitality.

In contrast to John, Marty realized that the problems, the conflicts, were within him. He then took steps to understand these problems and begin resolving them. John, on the other hand, dismissed the problem as Katherine, convincing himself that the right woman, a different woman, would provide the solution.

I am in no way saying that Marty's solution is always the right, the workable, one. Nor am I saying that divorce during this period is always wrong. What I am saying is that twenty years is a very large investment in something—large enough to warrant some effort to reap the dividends. Often, like Marty and Janice, you win. Sometimes, like Kurt and Elizabeth, you don't.

Elizabeth came to me with her mind made up. She was divorcing Kurt after twenty-five years of marriage. Their three children were grown, leaving just the two of them to enjoy all the dreams they had realized together. They had it all, supposedly. Kurt had the company vice-presidency he had worked toward for many long years. They had their first grandchild. They had the opportunity to travel to the most interesting places. In short, they had everything they had ever wanted in the early years of their marriage. But "everything," it seemed to Elizabeth now, was worth nothing.

Everything, in fact, had changed. Elizabeth had grown up. But Kurt had not. Elizabeth was growing, stretching. Kurt was staid and dull. Elizabeth wanted to experience more of life, to try new things, go to new places, try on new ideas. All Kurt wanted to do was watch TV and go to bed. Elizabeth was excited about life. Kurt, on the other hand, was just tired.

"I can't stand living with a dead person," Elizabeth told me. "Nothing is worth this price—not financial security, not our family life. I wake up so depressed I don't even want to get out of bed. Two years of begging, screaming, and begging some more have not helped. I want a divorce. I want to live my life."

Now, two years later, at age forty-seven, Elizabeth is doing just that. She has become a career woman who sees life as a great adventure. At forty-eight, Kurt, too, is a changed man, involved with many new and interesting people and activities. He finally understood what Elizabeth was asking for, albeit too late. He still loves Elizabeth. But she has now made a new life that has no room for him.

It took the crisis of the divorce to get Kurt to change. He had literally bypassed every growth stage, every crisis, between age twenty-nine and forty-five. But that was easy enough to hide in the whirlwind career climb and the din of three young children. It was not until the children were grown, the career goals reached, that the problem presented itself squarely: Elizabeth, in many ways, was living with a teenager. The unsolved problems rushed to the forefront. The "someday" Kurt and Elizabeth once dreamed of was here, and there was nothing of substance between them. There was nothing to sustain them through this most severe of crises.

If we have changed constantly, and in tandem, the relationship is far better equipped to weather the inevitable stresses of this twenty-year turning point. And the courage we have summoned, the honesty we have cultivated, the work we have done in the process give our relationship the strength to survive, and grow from, much more severe blows. This strength was revealed to me in the most personal of ways, by my sister Billie and her husband of more than twenty years, Robert.

With their youngest of three children finishing high school, Billie was eagerly anticipating the pleasure of being together with Robert once again, just the two of them. An extremely energetic man, Robert was literally on the go twelve hours a day either tackling one of his many responsibilities as school district superintendent or shooting a 79 on the golf course. Billie, too, was actively involved with her world—raising three children and caring for their home in the very largest sense of the word. But now, as these demands on their time began to ease, Billie and Robert were discovering a whole new world of opportunities—a world that they would now have more time to share with one another. But that world was shattered when Robert was involved in a serious automobile accident the very year they began truly to renew their relationship.

That was five years ago. And for those five years this giant of a man has lived in a body dead from the neck down. A severe spinal injury has robbed him of the use of everything but his head, his mind. But that is all he needed. Within six months of the accident, Robert resumed many of his duties as school district superintendent. By the end of the year, he was back at work full time. He exudes vitality, living as fully as possible within one of the greatest of limitations—a wheelchair.

Having watched their relationship develop, I know that this incredible courage, this capacity for life, is as much Billie's as it is Robert's. It is not his or hers really; it is theirs. When she looks at Robert, Billie does not see a handicapped person who is totally dependent upon her to meet the most basic of needs. She sees, instead, the dynamic man she has loved for more than twenty-five years, who still demands that she be involved with him, as he is with her. And that means, as it has throughout their relationship, complete involvement—sharing in feelings, in intimacy, in the love they have for one another. That does not mean that there were not periods of great distance between them; there were. Through the years the intensity of their feelings for one another has most surely ebbed and just as surely flowed back again. Their relationship has changed just as dramatically as Robert and Billie have changed over the last twenty-five years. They are no longer the exuberant youngsters who eagerly awaited their wedding day or the young parents who eagerly expected their first child or the couple of thirty eagerly rediscovering one another. They are not even the couple of five years ago who eagerly anticipated a very different future together. They are, though, still eager, and still anticipating. This year will bring Robert's retirement, and with it, a time when they will truly be together again, just the two of them.

INTO THE SUNSET

Robert and Billie are venturing into a world that I have never seen. I know its shape and terrain only from those who have gone ahead and shared the experience with me. From them I know of two worlds: one of great adventure and excitement, the other of resignation and bitterness. I know the entering of either to be a time of great crisis, for it is then that we begin our final reevaluation of our lives, of ourselves—if we dare. It is a period when great courage is required to confront the questions for which we must find answers, at least interim ones. We have done this essentially in every decade. But this time it is different. This time, we recognize, is perhaps our last opportunity to answer.

This retirement crisis is a time of choice, of change, and, ultimately, of freedom. It does not happen overnight, for retirement is more a process than an event. Ideally, it begins emotionally in our mid fifties when we begin retiring from the "shoulds" of life, begin exploring the "wants," and begin preparing emotionally for physical retirement at sixty-five or later. That early start gives us the time to begin shedding much of the now unnecessary baggage we have shouldered all our adult lives: duties, obligations, responsibilities. Shedding these shoulds is not easy because people keep telling you that you can't. You can.

Sam and Marion never believed that they could, let alone should. They had spent their entire lives frugally, working hard, spending little. Always feeling financially constrained, they constrained their lives as well. They knew how to work, how to save, how to suffer. But they did not know how to enjoy leisure time, money, themselves, each other. When they retired, Sam and Marion sold their real estate holdings and saw their financial worries disappear. No more scrimping and saving. No more overtime. Now what? They wanted to be free but could not shake a lifetime of living with the shoulds.

They tried traveling for a year, only to find that every time they left home, Marion became ill and Sam so anxious about what might be going wrong in their absence that he could not relax. After all, they had responsibilities. They had two married daughters (ages thirty-one and twenty-three) and three grandchildren to boot. They had Marion's mother (age seventy-eight). And they had a bachelor son (age twenty-six), who lived with them on and off. So they devoted most of their time to taking care of Marion's mother or baby-sitting for their grandchildren or preparing dinner for live-in son, Bruce.

It wasn't easy to convince Marion and Sam that they were imposing all these shoulds upon themselves, that, in fact, they had some choice in the matter. Yes, they finally acknowledged, their three children *were* adults. And yes, the grandchildren *were* their parents' responsibility. And yes, a twenty-six-year-old son *was* capable of cooking his own meals. And yes, Marion's mother *was* in excellent health and maintained her own apartment quite well, thank you. But still, they insisted, "What will happen to Mother when we are out of town? Who will check on her daily? Who will help her run errands? Who will take care of her if she is ill? Who will do Bruce's laundry? Who will make sure Bruce gets balanced meals? Who will take care of the grandchildren on weekends when their parents need to get away?"

You can see what I was up against. But helping this

couple free themselves from these "we shoulds" and begin living out the "we wants" was a great joy for me. In almost no time, I helped them accept their right to spend their money on themselves, on nonessential things, and truly enjoy the freedom and pleasures it brought them. One pleasure it brought them was the opportunity to pursue what had always been a favorite backyard hobby, bird-watching. They bought the freedom to go anywhere—a large motor home, which they christened My Life. They crisscrossed America, watching birds in the wild and people in the city. They traveled widely, spending on what pleased them. And they kept an apartment in their hometown so that they would have a place to come, when they chose, to be with family and friends.

They made their choices. But they were not without strong opposition. Their family, in fact, did everything in their power to burden Sam and Marion with guilt about these choices. And it worked for a while.

Sam and Marion did feel guilty, at first, about saying, "No, I'm sorry, but we can't baby-sit this weekend because we are going bird-watching," or, "No, Mother, I can't take you shopping this afternoon. I've already made other plans," or, "Well, Bruce, we'll be out of the house this evening, but I think I've seen a Laundromat right around the corner from you."

This family was furious with me for "ruining" their wonderful, loving parents. But I kept encouraging Marion and Sam to say yes only if they wanted to be with the grandchildren, not just because they felt they should. I encouraged them to help Marion's mother find her own friends and quit depending on them for her social life. And I insisted that they turn over responsibility for Bruce's life to Bruce.

Not only did Marion and Sam feel guilty about keeping their time to themselves; they also felt guilty about the money. Now, because I truly believe that it is up to each of us to make our own money as well as our own lives, I encouraged them to see that the money they had saved belonged to them, not their children. They finally decided that they deserved to do as they pleased with the money. They finally embraced their right to fun and relaxation. Marion and Sam finally freed themselves. No one else could do it for them. It was their responsibility to live as they truly wished and, ultimately, their only one.

That was six years ago. I still hear from Marion and Sam often enough to know that they have continued to want. This year they're taking French lessons because they want to tour the small towns in France. Last year they wanted to bird-watch in the Caribbean. The year before they wanted to spend a month exploring the California wilderness. They're doing it all. No explanations. No excuses. There is no time for that now. Time is too precious.

Retiring from the shoulds that have encumbered them during this period frees the couple to explore their wants. And sometimes retirement per se is the last thing they want. But continued work and productivity are not the sole answers to the questions that arise during this crisis period.

One couple who came to me in their mid sixties had no intention of retiring yet nonetheless were experiencing the crisis of this period in their relationship. Edward, a professional man, planned to continue his work throughout his life. He had made his choice. But now, with their three children grown, his wife, Lois, found herself facing only emptiness. After thirty-five years of marriage, there were no family responsibilities, no outside distractions, that Lois could hide her loneliness behind. It became increasingly difficult for Edward and Lois to pretend that the gulf between them did not exist. While Edward loved Lois deeply, he had never learned to share his thoughts and feelings with her. He did not trust that she would love him, would be on his side, would support him. Lois felt angry and estranged from Edward. She could not share her feelings with him. Sexual contact was rare because Lois felt so isolated.

It was this lack of sexual closeness that prompted Edward and Lois to seek help. They wanted to feel closer sexually. They wanted to live life with more intensity and creativity.

We began with Lois, helping her find, in her own way, a sense of vitality and meaning in life. She had always turned to Edward and the children to provide that excitement and meaning. She did not want to take the risks necessary to make her life her own. But, with Edward's encouragement, she began. At age sixty-four she opened a quilting shop with a close friend. As her own life took on new dimensions and became more truly hers, Lois became less angry with Edward for not giving her what she now realized only she could give herself. She began to want to feel closer to him, to see him not just as a provider but as a best friend and lover.

The closeness began with both Lois and Edward learning, in their mid sixties, to share with one another. Edward is learning to share his world with Lois. And Lois now has one of her own to offer in return.

For Sam and Marion, and Lois and Edward—each in their different way—retirement was a choice for life not death. For some people retirement means making this choice while you literally still can. I have met a number of men who chose to retire early because their jobs were killing them and they knew it. All have been highly successful, superachievers in their fields. One of these men, who retired at age sixty, was vice-president of a very large manufacturing firm. After forty years of hard work and high blood pressure, this man had finally made peace with his world. He and his wife enjoyed each other's company and had a real sense of love between them. They were not simply marking time but instead seeking out new adventures. They encouraged each other to discover new things: the pleasure of wood carving, the peace of long walks in the woods, the satisfaction of a garden.

Another couple, in their late sixties, I met on a float trip down the Snake River in Wyoming. I learned that since the husband's retirement, he had written two books on history—not for publication but for the pure pleasure of doing it. His wife had helped him and taken great pride in his accomplishments. There was a respect and a loving for each other built on forty-five years of marriage. They were having more fun than they had ever had in their lives. The man articulated their only regret: "We just wish we'd started twenty years ago!"

Another retired couple I knew lived in their motor home year round. Moving from a large, four-bedroom home in Michigan, they spend winters in Florida and summers traveling around the country. When they uprooted their lives four years ago, their children predicted a divorce within six months. But, instead of pulling them apart, the change has brought them closer. They have become more accepting of each other. Life had been a hard push for more than forty years. Now they had the freedom to pursue a completely different life-style, exciting and fresh.

Interestingly enough, all three of these retired men saw life as crippling, murderous, before they retired. All three expressed the feeling that if they had not quit working, they would not still be living.

And living they were. I remember those couples vividly because, unfortunately, they are the exception. I have found only a handful of retired couples, perhaps one in five, who want to live life with continued zest; who want to keep growing and maturing; who want to add to, not take away from, their lives; who, in their sixties and seventies, still welcome change and adventure. The remainder seek only to keep the thought of death at bay by not feeling too deeply. These couples, as they approach retirement, live increasingly in the here and now. They lose the intensity of feeling they once had. They concentrate on keeping busy to avoid feeling altogether. To avoid the thoughts of a sixty-five-year-old man: "I have worked all my life. My work is my *life*. My work is me." To avoid the musings of a sixty-year-old woman: "My children no longer need me. The house is empty. My purpose is gone." To avoid the final question: What am I to do with the rest of my life? What is left but death?

These are the people—the ones who try to protect themselves from that last, terrible question of death—who become diminished and bitter. The fear of death relates decidedly to not living life. If we have lived life fully and continue to do so, death holds no fear for us. It is only if we have not been and are not now truly living that death is a horror.

My two closest friends died in their forties, about a year apart. Bobby had always feared life, had shrunk back, had cheated himself emotionally. Patrick, in contrast, relished life, ran toward it, embraced all the joy and sorrow it had to offer. When Bobby died, I truly grieved for him, for he had never lived. For Patrick, I felt only thankfulness that he had had so very much.

While death, as the antithesis of life, is always with us, it is the couple over sixty who must confront this ultimate crisis most directly. It is for these couples that the courage to face the finality of this crisis openly and honestly is most difficult, that the honesty is the most elusive, that the work is most poignant.

It is for them, too, that the final rewards of a lifetime of journeying, of becoming, with another human being can be the greatest.

Sam and Marion realized this when they came to me asking for only one thing: "Help us learn how to live. Even if it takes us two solid years to learn to live for one single day, that is enough. Give us hope that we can change, that we can cheat death—not life."

7

Something More

"Give us hope that we can change." It is this persistent and powerful hope, which each of you somehow brought to this book, that I want most of all to affirm. It is hope that you can learn to live with more vitality, more adventure, more joy; hope that you can love with more honesty, more involvement, more intensity. It is hope, in short, that there is "more"—and hope that you can have it.

"More," in fact, is what most of you were looking for when you picked up this book: more from your marriage, more from your spouse, more from yourself. In these pages I have tried to encourage you to want that "more"—more sharing, more caring, more intimacy, more security, more everything—*very* much. Because how much more you *get* relates decidedly to how much you *want* and how much *work* you are willing to put in.

Most of you *are* willing to work for what you want. So, in this book, I have tried to share with you some of the basic skills, the techniques, that foster growth and change and progression in a relationship: talking, sharing, listening, caring, graffling, exploring, loving.

I have shared them because I have faith in your *courage* to use them, to go for broke in your relationship, to welcome change in spite of your fears. I have faith in your *honesty*, in your refusal to cheat yourself or deny your true feelings or settle for second best. I have faith in your determination to *work;* to learn and practice your newfound skills; to keep reaching, to keep demanding, even when you are very, very tired. I have faith in your commitment to *change*, to growth, to life. I have faith in your *love* for each other.

And most of you *do* love each other. Most of you began this book with that basic ingredient, the one for which there can be no substitutions. Hopefully, you have found in this book a new way of expressing that love for your spouse, a new way of understanding your lives together. You have learned something not about love but about loving.

THE FIRST STEP

You have acquired some tools, some techniques, for loving that you may not have had before. These are tools that may help you clear a path where none can be found and techniques that may keep you from turning back, from protecting, from pretending, from "settling," or from just plain giving up.

How you may use these techniques is up to you. There are no right or wrong ways of relating and loving; there are only ways that work and do not work. And they are not the same for any two couples, for each couple is as unique as the two individuals who comprise it—individuals who want and need unique things in a unique way. It is from each individual that the hope and desire for something more springs. And it is within each individual, within you, that the courage to work toward it can be found.

I say courage because, remember, true courage is

only necessary when we are afraid. To do something we do not fear requires no courage. And sometimes in our marriage, we *are* afraid. We are afraid to feel openly, afraid to speak honestly, afraid to change. This is understandably so. Marriage is the most vital of all our relationships. We don't want to take chances with it. So our fear holds us back and encourages us to protect ourselves and our partner from our doubts and disappointments, to even pretend that they don't exist, perhaps. It encourages us to settle for what we have instead of what we want.

But this fear can be very informative. It is an index that should tell you something important about yourself, about your spouse, about your marriage. If you are afraid, start first by examining your fear. What are you afraid of anyway? What *would* you be risking, for instance, by being honest about your feelings and discussing them openly with your partner? A loss of intimacy? Or financial security? Or sexual closeness? Once you know what you're afraid of jeopardizing, or losing, your fear is an index of just how important that particular aspect of your relationship is to you, what its *value* in your life is. If you don't stand to lose much—say, by telling your spouse that you don't like the way he or she squeezes the toothpaste tube—the fear does not handicap you, and you just speak up! But if you are risking something very important, very valuable—say, by telling your partner that you do not experience him or her as loving or sexually inviting— you're dealing with a totally different type of fear. You're dealing with the kind that can be almost crippling.

It takes tremendous courage to move forward in spite of this fear. And if protecting or pretending or loafing or resisting change has become an established pattern in a relationship, the first step is the hardest. It requires the courage to begin, with one act or word, to live honestly and openly, to begin freeing yourself and your spouse from the tethers that you have put on your relationship.

Once we have begun, once we see from experience that honesty and work and change will not destroy our marriage but revitalize it, the process gets easier. Not easy, just easier! It still takes that old "gutting up" to get past our fears of hurt, rejection, and mis-understanding and to get on with the truth. But once we have built a foundation of positive experience using these techniques, we are not as fearful anymore that we will be destructive or be destroyed. We dis-cover that we are constructive instead. And that posi-tive experience provides the impetus for continued honesty and work and change. Just as destructive processes—protecting, pretending, loafing—tend to perpetuate themselves, so the positive processes do as well. The trick is to establish some positive momen-tum. Sometimes that means stopping a full-steam negative swing and setting it in motion in a totally different direction. And this is the most difficult, the most threatening, but often the most necessary, step of all.

Sometimes, some of you, even with your love for one another, may find it impossible to muster the courage that it takes. You may need some help setting that positive swing in motion. Some of you may find that you have the courage but do not really know how to go about working and changing. You may need help learning how to foster growth in your relation-ship. Some of you may realize that you don't know how to be *loving*, that you don't know how to express your love in a way your spouse can understand it. You may need help in learning how to communicate your love. Some of you may find that you have lost the path at one of marriage's crossroads and need a guide to help you find your way back.

If you find yourself at any of these impasses, it may be time for you to seek some professional help. This is particularly true during the crisis periods, the crossroads, in a marriage. Too often we fall back on our old beliefs that marriage is instinctive, automatic, natural—that we don't need any training or education to learn how to relate to our spouse. Yet this kind of training can be our most important investment. When people realize that loving someone, sharing and caring, is something you learn how to do, they will seek this education from a trained teacher, a guide if you will, more readily.

THERAPY IS NOT A DIRTY WORD

For the most part, when we stray off course in this journeying we call marriage, we are strong enough, courageous enough, honest enough, and determined enough to get ourselves back on track. But sometimes when the fear is too great, or the fog too thick, a trained guide can be of great value in helping us move forward.

At present far too many people think of therapy as being for the very sick, for those who are unable to function in life. Certainly, we need, and have, excellent treatment teams and hospitals to handle individuals with severe, almost crippling, emotional disorders. But the vast majority of people who seek therapy or marriage counseling do not need tranquilizers or hospitalization. In fact, often they do not *need* anything, in the traditional sense. But they do *want* something more, something better from their lives and from their relationships. These people see therapy as an opportunity for growth.

Therapy is for those people who are not satisfied with just getting by, with just existing. It is for those who really want to live—who want to free themselves from the constraints that hold them back, both individually and in their important relationships. It is for those who want to live life with more openness and joy. In short, therapy is *not* for those who are basically unsuccessful. It is for the successful who want to add to their lives, who are willing to invest in them, who recognize that they must put something into life to get something back. What these people *want*—and, yes, sometimes need—is a therapist who can help them find their own methods, not molds, for improving their life, for making it uniquely theirs, for reaping the benefits and accepting the consequences.

Many people fear that a therapist will mold them into a certain kind of person, one well equipped to handle any situation, spouting all the right psychological lingo. A good therapist does not mold people. He or she has no preconceived notion of how the patient (you!) should "turn out." Yet many individuals come into therapy looking to the therapist for the magic answer, saying, "Tell me what to do. I'll do anything you say." They try to give their therapist the responsibility for "curing" them. I, and any other good therapist, will have none of this. I inform these people, in no uncertain terms, that there are no magic answers, that therapy is a cooperative experience in which we work together to find the answers for them.

It would be a boring life indeed for me if I did not see each new person, or couple, as unique; if I did not embark with them on a great adventure, for a destination even I could not guess; if I did not serve, basically, as a guide, helping each couple chart their own unique course.

The therapist does not draw a map, charting the patient's path from point A through point B all the way to point Z. In therapy, as in marriage, there is no predetermined end point. Therapy merely facilitates a process of becoming that continues throughout a person's life. It is primarily a learning experience, a means of acquiring knowledge about ourselves. It is a process by which we discover the truth—what it is *for us,* how to speak of it, how to live by it. I say "discover" because often we have denied our true feelings—our joys, our fears, our wishes, our disappointments—so long that we have buried them. Digging them up is the first step. Then comes speaking of them, first with the therapist—who will accept, who will not judge, who will understand. In speaking of how we truly feel, what we truly want, we begin to determine the course we wish to take. We begin the becoming process. When we have summoned the courage and mastered the techniques to speak honestly, even to graffle, with the therapist, we can begin to take these skills and apply them in other relationships.

IN SEARCH OF A GUIDE

But finding the right person to help, when you need help, is critical. There are several types of what I call helping professionals who, by virtue of their training and experience, are technically qualified to serve as guides. And they fall into three major categories: psychiatrists, psychologists, and social workers. These three differ in terms of training and licensing. A psychiatrist has a degree in medicine and is licensed by the state. However, you should be aware that a medical doctor licensed as a psychiatrist is not required to have completed a three-year residency at a certified hospital. So it is important to determine whether the psychiatrist you are considering has this post–medical school training. And often the only way you can find out is to ask. Psychiatrists with this training may be certified by the American Board of Psychiatry and Neurology. Furthermore, some psychiatrists have received additional training in psychoanalytic modes of therapy and have been certified by the American Psychoanalytic Association.

Psychiatrists are required to be licensed to practice in any and all states—not so psychologists and social workers. Many states have no licensing procedures for these two categories of helping professionals. That means that in these states *anyone* can represent himself or herself as a psychologist or social worker. But if your state does have a licensing law, certain basic educational and clinical experiences are required before an individual can hang out either one of these two "shingles." A clinical psychologist is trained in clinical psychology, not in experimental psychology, industrial psychology, or anything else. He or she should possess a doctoral degree from an accredited institution and, if applicable, be licensed by the state. A social worker should have a master's degree in social work and must have passed a board examination for certification as a clinical social worker. He or she may be a member of the Academy of Certified Social Workers (ACSW). A social worker may also be licensed by the state as a clinical social worker or social psychotherapist. Registration for qualified clinical social workers is provided in the National Registry of Health Care Providers in Clinical Social Work.

What is the difference between these three types of helping professionals? Basically, all three of these groups are trained to approach and deal with marital problems in essentially the same way. While social workers have been specifically trained to work with families, psychiatrists and psychologists, who in the past focused primarily on the individual, have become increasingly interested in this field during the past decade. Today all three of these specialists are interested in marriage counseling and are specifically trained to provide it.

In addition to the type of therapist, fees are an

inevitable consideration in choosing a counselor. Today fees for therapists in private practice range from $25 to $100 for each forty-five-minute session, depending on the part of the country in which you live and on the educational background and experience of the therapist. That sounds like a lot of money. And it is. Therapy for six months as a couple may run about $2,500, and yet that is half of what you might spend on a car or living-room furniture. It is an investment that will pay dividends for the rest of your life. I'm not saying that it is an investment to make casually. What I am saying is that if you and your partner *need* and *want* the benefits of counseling in terms of a more open, honest, loving relationship, a price tag should not be the deciding factor.

But if economics are a primary consideration, there are certainly sources of counseling other than the private therapist. In most communities there are agencies that charge for services according to a patient's ability to pay. And therapists practicing in these agencies are many times just as good—or just as bad!—as those in private practice. These agencies are generally supported by the United Fund or a governmental body. Your United Fund information service, your local Mental Health Association, or your doctor or religious leader can help you find these agencies in your area and tell you what services they provide.

One final consideration: the type of therapy. There are usually four ways of working on a marriage relationship through therapy. These may be used by a therapist individually or in combination with one another, depending on the patient's needs and the patient's response to each type. The most common and familiar form of therapy is the one-on-one variety called individual therapy, in which the therapist works alone with a single individual. In conjoint therapy a single therapist counsels both partners together. Another method, called dual therapy, involves a male and female cotherapist team working with the couple. Each session involves the four participants' learning to work together. While this latter method is the one I use most often because of the quick results, it may be impossible if only one partner is willing to seek counseling. For the spouse who does enter therapy, it is important to remember that as he or she changes, the more reluctant partner will inevitably change in response.

Group therapy is a fourth method, often used in concert with one of the other three. A therapy group is made up of a maximum of ten people who meet for one or two hours each week. These are people learning how to be more open with people other than their therapist, who monitors the group. They are learning how to quit protecting and pretending. They are learning how to work and change. They are learning how to communicate: to talk and listen. They are, in essence, practicing their newfound skills in a protected environment with one or more therapists present. Often group therapy is a follow-up for individual, conjoint, or dual therapy, a place to stamp in the progress made as a couple.

With all these things to think about, it may seem like an overwhelming task to find the right therapist, the guide who has the educational training and the approach that will most help you and your spouse. Far easier it is to give in to your fear and say, "It's just too much trouble. I'll just be wasting my time and money." The hardest part is beginning, admitting that you want some help at whatever time for whatever reason. And the easiest place to start, and often the best, is with a friend or acquaintance who has been in therapy and in whom you have seen some positive changes, some indication that he or she has been helped by a therapist. Individuals who have been in therapy are your best source of referral to a competent guide. They can also probably tell you about their experience, thus easing your natural apprehension or anxiety about seeking counseling. However, if you don't know anyone who has been in or through therapy, your best sources of referral are your family physician, religious leader, or the Mental Health Association or United Fund information service in your area.

But the most important consideration in choosing a therapist is how you feel about him or her. Do you like the guide you have chosen? Do you feel that he or she likes you? can help you? You are the only person who can evaluate this particular relationship. If you find that the therapist you have chosen initially is *not* someone you like or can trust, run—don't walk—to another therapist. Ask the one you are seeing to suggest another, or go back to your original referral source. Once you are sure that you have located the right guide for you, someone you like and trust, roll up your shirt sleeves. You've got a lot of work to do, and a good therapist won't do it for you.

A therapist, then, is not a teacher. You, yourself, are both teacher and student, for only you can decide what course, what direction, you will take. A therapist's job is to help you discover the knowledge that will give you the freedom to do just that. This knowledge provides the confidence and the power to shape your life in a way that is right, that works, for you and you alone. It is when that knowledge is complete enough that you, as an individual or a couple, are equipped with the understanding, the techniques, and the courage you need to continue the journey alone, that the therapist's job is done.

SETTING YOUR OWN COURSE

With or without a guide, it is you alone who must decide what you want from yourself, from your spouse, from your relationship. And wanting, really, is the basis of loving, of striving, of growing, of living— wanting something more, something closer, something richer.

Does that sound selfish? I hope so, because loving is, and should be, for the self as well as for others. Loving, as we discussed from the beginning of this book, is not self-sacrificing but self-fulfilling. Sharing and caring and relating and loving all involve giving as well as receiving. They require a giver and a receiver, a lover and a beloved, a me and a you wanting to give, wanting to receive, wanting each other.

So I encourage your wanting something more today than you had yesterday, something less than you'll have tomorrow. If you're working, if you're changing, if you're growing, there will always be something more.

ABOUT THE AUTHORS

MARLENE LAROE received a Masters Degree in Psychiatric Social Work from Smith College in 1953. She then spent two years at a VA hospital in Medical Rehabilitation, another two at the Polio Foundation as Assistant Director of Social Services, and a number of years as Director of Special Projects, Family Service Bureau. Recently Ms. LaRoe held the positions of Associate Professor of Sociology at Sam Houston State, and lecturer at the University of Houston. She has also been a visiting lecturer on sexual dysfunctioning therapy at the Graduate School of Social Work, University of Houston and on couples therapy at the University of Texas Medical School. Ms. LaRoe has been in private practice as a Social Psychotherapist since 1959, specializing in family and sexual dysfunctioning therapies.

LEE HERRICK is a Houston writer who has published primarily in the health field.

THE FAMILY—TOGETHER AND APART

Choose from this potpourri of titles for the information you need on the many facets of family living.

☐ 12296	**THE FUTURE OF MARRIAGE** Jessie Bernard	$2.75
☐ 14211	**LOVE AND SEX IN PLAIN LANGUAGE** Eric W. Johnson	$1.95
☐ 14486	**THE PLEASURE BOND** Masters & Johnson	$3.50
☐ 14217	**DARE TO DISCIPLINE** J. Dobson	$2.50
☐ 13164	**A PARENT'S GUIDE TO CHILDREN'S READING** Nancy Larrick	$2.50
☐ 13258	**P.E.T. IN ACTION** Thomas Gordon with J. Gordon Sands	$2.75
☐ 12632	**LOVE AND SEX AND GROWING UP** Johnson & Johnson	$1.75
☐ 12906	**THE BOYS AND GIRLS BOOK ABOUT DIVORCE** Richard A. Gardner	$1.95
☐ 12567	**THE NEW BIRTH CONTROL PROGRAM** Garfink & Pizer	$2.50
☐ 11378	**HOW TO GET IT TOGETHER WHEN YOUR PARENTS ARE COMING APART** Richards & Willis	$1.75
☐ 12821	**ANY WOMAN CAN** David Reuben, M.D.	$2.50
☐ 13624	**NAME YOUR BABY** Lareina Rule	$2.25
☐ 13773	**YOU AND YOUR WEDDING** Winnifred Gray	$2.95
☐ 11365	**OF WOMAN BORN: Motherhood as Experience and Institution** Adrienne Rich	$2.95

Buy them at your local bookstore or use this handy coupon for ordering:

Bantam
On Psychology

☐	13721	**PASSAGES: Predictable Crises of Adult Life,** Gail Sheehy	$3.50
☐	13886	**PEACE FROM NERVOUS SUFFERING,** Claire Weekes	$2.50
☐	13842	**THE GESTALT APPROACH & EYE WITNESS TO THERAPY,** Fritz Perls	$2.95
☐	11656	**KICKING THE FEAR HABIT,** Manuel J. Smith	$2.25
☐	14324	**THE BOOK OF HOPE,** DeRosis & Pellegrino	$2.95
☐	14393	**THE PSYCHOLOGY OF SELF-ESTEEM: A New** Concept of Man's Psychological Nature, Nathaniel Branden	$2.95
☐	14311	**WHAT DO YOU SAY AFTER YOU SAY HELLO?** Eric Berne, M.D.	$2.95
☐	14201	**GESTALT THERAPY VERBATIM,** Fritz Perls	$2.75
☐	14480	**PSYCHO-CYBERNETICS AND SELF-FULFILLMENT,** Maxwell Maltz, M.D.	$2.75
☐	13518	**THE FIFTY-MINUTE HOUR,** Robert Lindner	$2.25
☐	13080	**THE DISOWNED SELF,** Nathaniel Branden	$2.50
☐	11756	**CUTTING LOOSE: An Adult Guide for Coming to Terms With Your Parents,** Howard Halpern	$2.25
☐	14372	**BEYOND FREEDOM AND DIGNITY,** B. F. Skinner	$3.50
☐	13715	**WHEN I SAY NO, I FEEL GUILTY,** Manuel Smith	$2.95
☐	12837	**IN AND OUT OF THE GARBAGE PAIL** Fritz Perls	$2.50

Buy them at your local bookstore or use this handy coupon for ordering:

WE DELIVER!

And So Do These Bestsellers.

Bantam Book Catalog

Here's your up-to-the-minute listing of over 1,400 titles by your favorite authors.

This illustrated, large format catalog gives a description of each title. For your convenience, it is divided into categories in fiction and non-fiction—gothics, science fiction, westerns, mysteries, cookbooks, mysticism and occult, biographies, history, family living, health, psychology, art.

So don't delay—take advantage of this special opportunity to increase your reading pleasure.

Just send us your name and address and 50¢ (to help defray postage and handling costs).